THE GOLDEN RANGE

By IRA A. COLE

Copyright © 2023 Ira A. Cole
All rights reserved.
ISBN-13: 979-8-218-33171-9

"In the picture you can tell that the parents, Fayette and Susan Gentry Cole are seated in the center front. My grandfather--your great grandfather, John Newton is at the left of Fayette. The men in back are--from left to right, Jacob (Jake), Cassius (Cass), Gilbert (Gil), and James (Jim). I'm pretty sure the lady in the center back is our Aunt Jenny. I vaguely remember her. The one in white is Aunt Effie. I have always heard that she was the contrary one with a strong will and mind of her own, and the white dress seems to prove it out since all the others are dressed in dark clothes."

Rose Cole Shepherd, Dec. 7, 1986

Children of John and Tilla C. (Tate) Cole: (left to right) Rose Meyers, Gene, Gladys Hurst, Grace Floyd (later Carey), Warren, Pern Turner, Ira, Lula Ferguson. (Summer 1916)

The four remaining Cole brothers about 1940): Cass, Jake, Gil, and Jim.

Table of Contents

Foreword vi
1. The Coles 1
2. Pap 12
3. Some Sons-in-Law 20
4. "I won't bump the rub!" 26
5. Concerning the Autumn 33
6. About Some Horses and Their Riders 38
7. Concerning Geese, Wild and Otherwise 47
8. Some Landmarks 52
9. About the Springtime 56
10. About Some Neighbors 61
11. The Baileys 68
12. Ante Bellum Days 76
13. Some Philosophy and Other Things 82
14. Therapeutics of the Plains 88
15. More Wild Flowers 94
16. Uncle Zeke's Duel 99
17. Philosophy, Hodgepodge, and 'Bunker Hill' 105
18. About the Night 112
19. Life, Cattle, Sheep - and Jim 118
20. Wild Horses and Wilder Men 124
21. Uncle Oll 131
22. Some Prairie Inventors 136
23. About the Knapps 142
24. The Beloved Physician 149
25. The Scotts 154
26. Old Fort Zimmerman 159
27. The Passing Show 163
28. Curley 173
29. Tan, Lizzy and the Teater Kids 181
30. Along the Creek 187
31. A Day's Work 193
Epilogue 201

Foreword

The stories of those settling the plains of western Kansas are at once inspiring as well as challenging. They remind us of an era and an area where the luxuries we take for granted such as instantly available water (and indoor plumbing!), pillows, and plenty of indoor space were non-existent, or incredibly difficult to obtain, even if they did exist in other, more established areas.

This collection of stories, written by my 2nd great-grandfather, Ira A. Cole, about his grandfather, my 4th great-grandfather, represent a colorful view of life in late 1800s western Kansas. The stories are varied in the aspects of life they cover, and it certainly is possible that some of them are yarns. But if you choose to look closer, you will find that the names mentioned are very real. I have included a couple images of a 1901 Ness County property map that show owners of various sections of Ness County, near Bazine. As you read the stories, go find the family names on the maps. There are many!

This work was first created in 1961. As far as I know, Ira never had it published. I am in possession, as are some of my extended family, of a typed version of this manuscript, that I believe was created by Rose Cole Shepherd, in 1986. Rose was born on the golden range, in Bazine, Kansas, in 1918, as the 5th child of Ira Cole and his wife Myra (Burnett). She passed in 2017, not seeing the full publishing of this work.

I am uncertain of exactly when or how I came into possession of this copy of the manuscript. It has sat on my bookshelf for at least a decade. For a period of time, I would pull it out every Saturday evening and read a chapter to my kids and a group of friends as we sat around the table, or around the firepit in the backyard. We would laugh at the funny stories. We would discuss life on the prairie. It was a great time.

My goal in publishing this work is to preserve the history of settlement of western Kansas, as well as pass these stories on to my own children. They, and you, will benefit from understanding the struggles and the joys that our ancestors went through. We stand on their shoulders today.

A word of caution for the reader: The language used in this book is a product of the era and the environment the author and his family were raised in: southern plantation life. Words are used that we would not speak today. In publishing this, I did not edit the language, or even correct the spelling. I wrestled with this and chose not to soften history. While we certainly own the sins of our past – that they happened, and how they happened, is more of a matter of fact, than of preference for our current day and age.

Lastly, I encourage you to read Ira A Cole's other published works, including *The Golden Antelope* and *Ibe of Atlan*. In addition, you may find various poems written and published by Ira. He wrote prolifically and was friends with people such as Howard Phillips Lovecraft. In fact, an article by R. Alain Everts notes their friendship describing Ira as, "a former cowboy and uneducated plainsman, the man HPL described as "a strange and brilliant character—an utterly illiterate ranchman and ex-cowboy of Western Kansas who possesses a streak of brilliant poetic genius." H.P. Lovecraft mentored Ira in poetic writing, which surely contributed to this book.

I hope you enjoy these stories as much as I have!

-Philip Snell

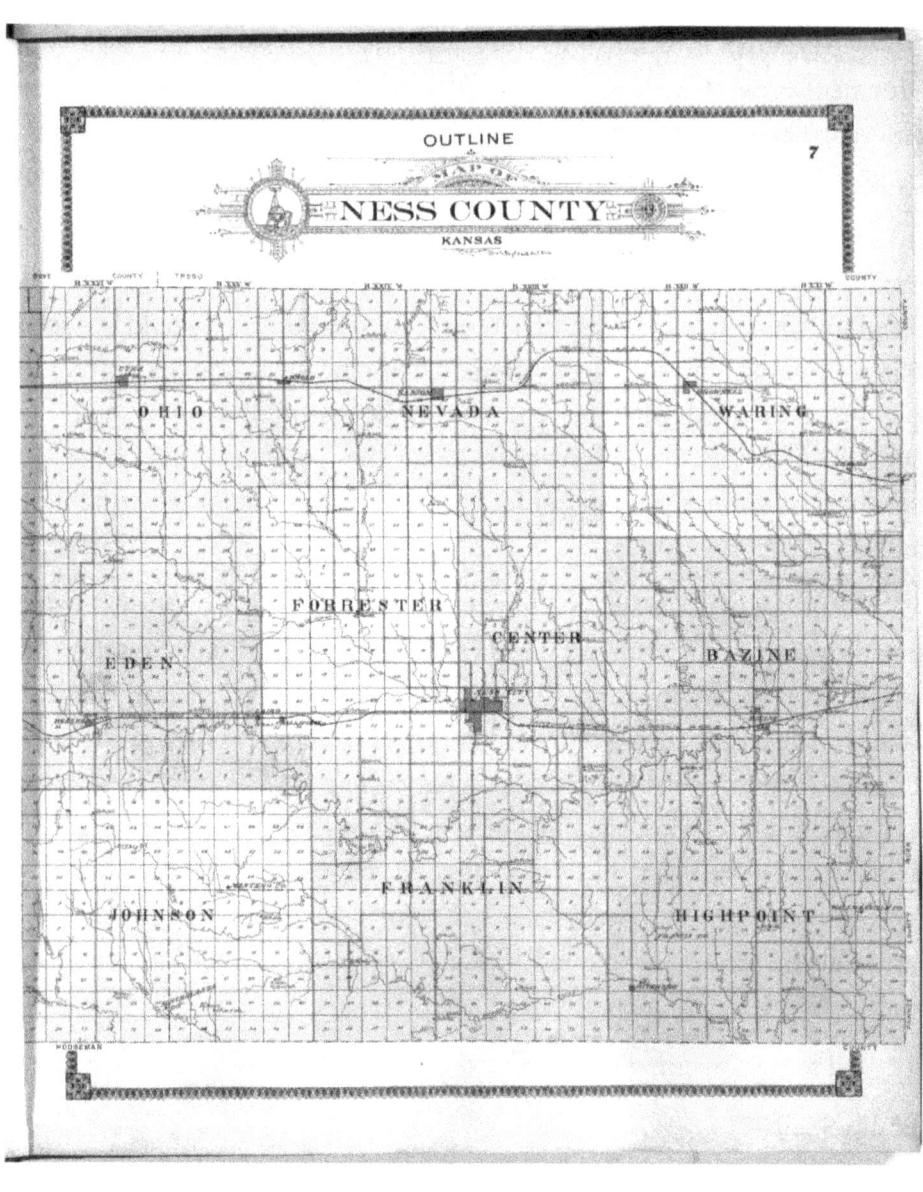

1901 Map of Ness County Kansas

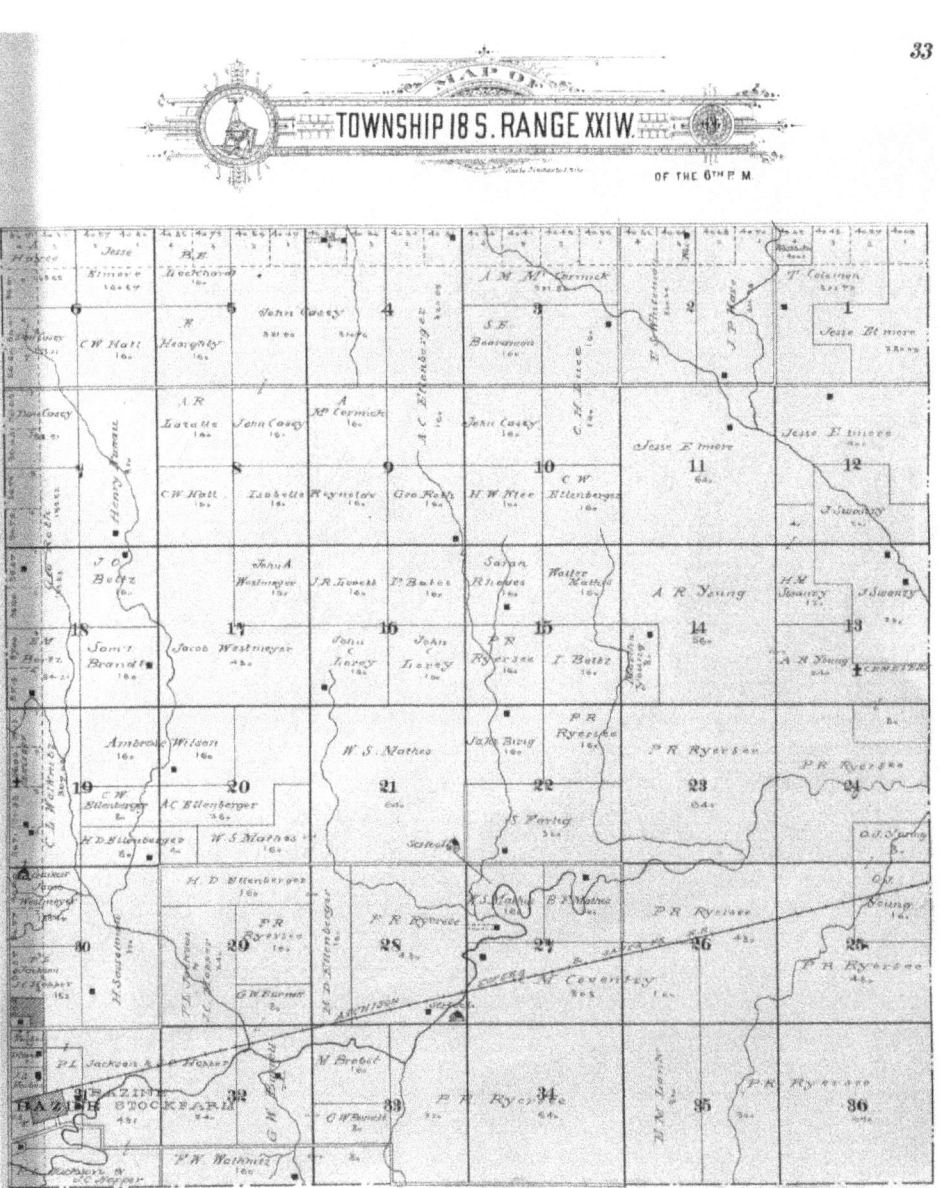

Map of sections to the northeast of Bazine

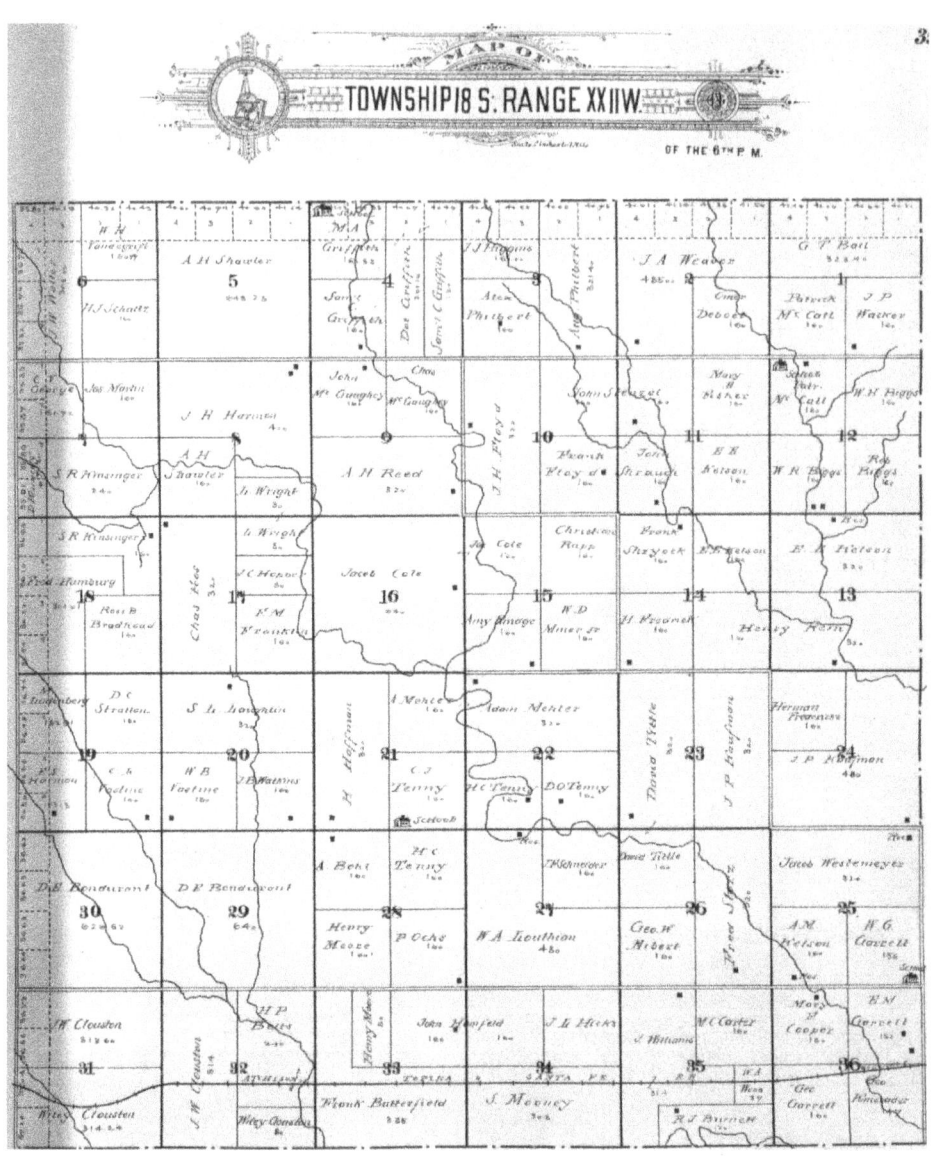

Map of the sections to the northwest of Bazine

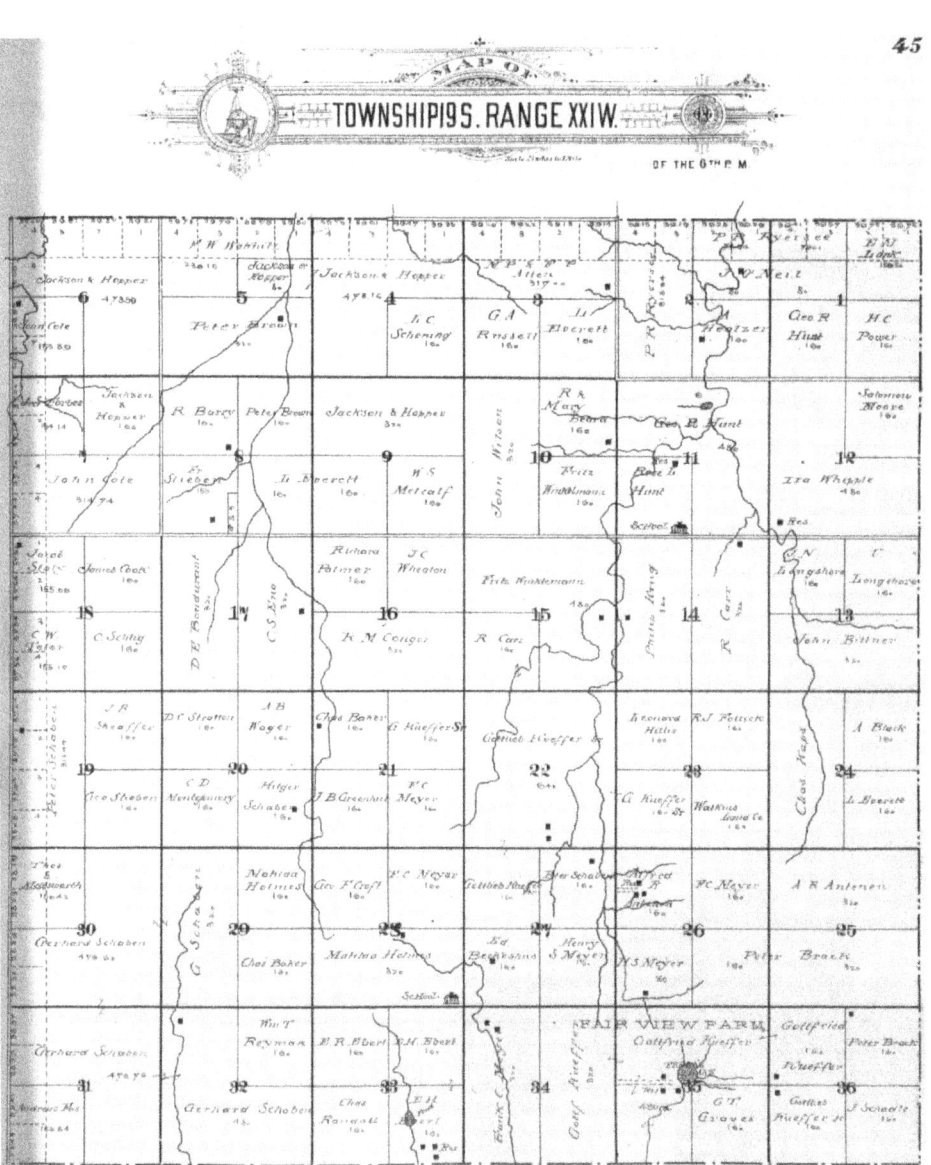

Map of the sections to the southeast of Bazine

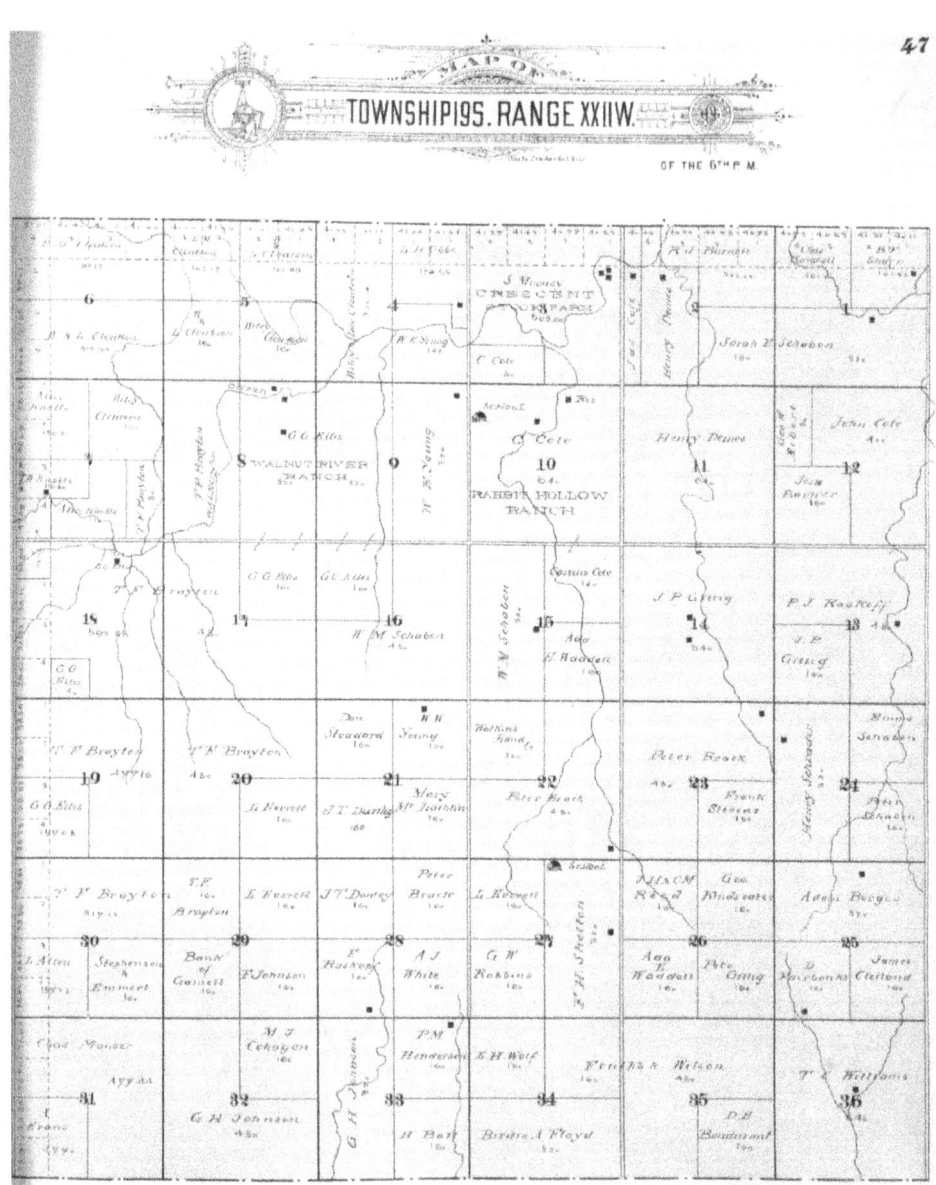

Map of the sections to the southwest of Bazine

Satellite image of Bazine and land north, with Cole property highlighted.

Satellite image of Bazine and land south, with Cole property highlighted.

1. The Coles

There were fourteen of them, counting the half-breed Indian boy, plus one foot-sore dog, seven horses and an old spotted cow with just a piece of a tail. At the command, "Whoa!", the horses stopped and the off sorrel mare reached down and began to gather the soft, brown prairie grass in great hungry mouthfuls. The heavily loaded Jackson wagons creaked to a halt.

Out in front, the old man leaned on his cane stared out a long moment across the land, and then turned to the waiting group. His eyes glowed, and when he spoke, his voice shook just a little.

'Take 'em out, boys, an' give 'em a little grass."

"You mean...?"

"I mean...this is hit!"

You sure, Pap? All of this! From here, way off yonder to the top of that big hill 'bout twenty miles away?"

"Yep, Jenny," the old man said, smiling down at the girl. "This is hit. Just as far as you can see... and a great deal further. From here clear on acrost the Arkansas River, and even down into Texas an' acrost the Rio Grande!

"The Golden Range!" His voice softened with memory, "That's what General Kearney called it thirty years ago when we came this way goin' down into the Gila Bend country. That's what the Mormon boys called it, too. The Golden Range! Sure looked like gold to us then. I ain't never been able to forget it. A while here an' you won't either."

He turned his sharp eyes on them, weighing, evaluating. "Wait 'til spring...when the flowers are all in bloom. Then you'll know what I mean.

Chapter 1: The Coles

Go away, like I did, an' you won't be happy... until you come back. Sleep here one night an' there'll never be another home on earth for you."

They listened in silence, a little awed by the old man's words, unable as yet to understand the intense emotion which they sensed was running deep within him.

"You boys are all young," he continued. "Well, this is a young country. An' this Golden Range, this prairie land, is like the Golden Age of the Ancients. The moment I shouted 'Whoa!' an' the horses stopped you became a part of this land. You're going to grow to love it as I do. You're going to have the best time of your lives here. An' like me, you'll never be free of it. Mark me well!"

These were my people, these fourteen, and even the dog and the pony horses seem somehow a part of me...so often have heard them spoken of and their adventures recounted.

This was Kansas and the Golden Range, as the old man called it. Around them, the new world of prairie grass stretched away on every side, with never a house nor a fence to hinder or grieve the eye.

It was October 26, 1878.

They were tired, bone-tired all of them. Road weary from the stretch of miles that lay across the great country from Independence, Missouri to this Golden Range of western Kansas. Only the old man seemed enthused by the prospects around him. The young people, worn out by their three hundred mile walk, had little to say this first evening of their lives on the Golden Range.

On the wagon seat, the woman began gathering up the knitting with which she had occupied herself during the weary hours and long miles that lay behind. Now, as if a new day had dawned, she tucked it away in the box beside her and stood up.

Chapter 1: The Coles

"Well, I do say there seems to be plenty of it, this Golden Range of yours," she said dryly. Then: "Come, Lizzie, the rest of you girls! Get that camp outfit gain!! We got to eat... even if we have reached the land of promise!"

The boys, seven of them, soon had the tired horses unharnessed and grazing on the short grass. Water was brought from a nearby buffalo wallow and put to boil in a great copper kettle over a chip fire.

"Always boil your water," cautioned the old man. "Kearney taught us that trick when we passed this way before. An' not a mother's son of us got sick from the water. But some of the Mormon boys sure had a time of it. Typhoid, dysentery an' God knows what not. Couldn't take time from their prayers to boil their water! Me... I think God means for folks to kind of help themselves a little, 'stead of askin' so much from Him."

"Pap, do folks have the shakes here on the Golden Range?" Effie Lee, the youngest of the girls, asked worriedly. In Missouri, the shakes, or chills and 'ague., Was quite common... and Effie Lee had had her share of the trouble.

"I don't think so, " the old man replied, "'What do you say, Jim?' He turned to the Cherokee boy who Was standing nearby. "Any of your people ever had the shakes?"

"Not in this country, sir." Jim was always very courteous in his manners toward older people... always calling them Mr. and Mrs. and Sir, as the case might be.

"My people used to come to these uplands when the fevers got bad along the rivers. They always got well from their sickness."

"Well, I sure hope I don't have any more shakes," sniffed Effie Lee. "It would be heaven just to be free of 'em for one whole summer!"

"Pap, why do folks call this the Golden Range?" Cleopatry, one of

Chapter 1: The Coles

the older girls, broke the temporary silence. "I haven't seen any gold yet. An' I been lookin' ever since we left the river three days ago. What is gold about it? Unless it be the afternoon sun!"

The old man smiled tolerantly, content in this moment to let them talk, and to answer their questions as best he could.

"It's gettin' pretty late in the year for the gold to show," he said. "But come spring an' all these flowers will bloom...along with the other wild flowers along the ridge here and on the gumbo flats, further back toward the divide. He stared quietly out across the land, his eyes bright with memory.

"I'll never forget that summer, thirty years ago when we came across the creek back there and first saw these prairies. I was riding with the General an' some Indian scouts who had brought us on ahead to find the ford across the creek. Suddenly we came out of the bottoms past that lone cottonwood back there and out on the prairies." He caught his breath, and when he continued, his voice was husky with emotion.

"Just one big flower garden from here clear to the horizon! Most of it yellow sunflower, with here an' there a bunch of buffalo or antelope grazing about. An' some wild horses, too!

"The Golden Range!' the General said softly. 'Did you ever see a fairer sight, Cole?'

"An' even remembering the Shenandoah and the Blue Ridge, I had to admit it was the prettiest sight I'd ever looked upon. An' right there before the General, I made a covenant with myself to come back some day an' settle down for good. How, here I am... an' here I mean to stay!"

Busy over the cooking pots, his wife, Susan, spoke in a practical voice. "For the life of me, I can't figure how you are going to feed fourteen people on scenery! Even if it be golden in the springtime as you say. For

Chapter 1: The Coles

my part, I'm already homesick for the hills of ole Virginia!"

"Well, now, Virginia is a good long way back there. An' I, for one, mean never to see it again," pap retorted. "If we can't make it here., I'll just starve an' be done with it. At least, Susan, I'll die with plenty of pretty scenery around me!"

"I'll not have you talk about Virginia that way!" Susan said indignantly.

"Oh, Virginia was all right," the old man said easily, "until the damned Yankees came along an' ruined it. This, now, is a new country. I don't mean there shall be any Yankee or Confederate either on the Golden Range. Just plenty of plain American folks with no Mason-Dixon line between 'em. An' just a good neighborly feelin' reachin' out to everybody that comes along."

"Don't seem like anybody's going to come along," said Jenny, one of the older, unmarried girls, in obvious dissatisfaction. "Haven't seen a soul except ourselves since we left them Yankee soldiers three days ago. Unless you call old man Harvey at Alexander a soul, which I doubt very much!"

"Now don't get yourself all worked up, Jenny." John, the oldest and the only married one of the boys, said good naturedly. "I bet a quarter it won't be twenty-four hours before you're makin' eyes at some gander-shanks who'll come slippin' through the grass 'round here. An' whether he has a soul or not won't much matter!"

I do like it here," Jenny admitted. "An' I mean to be like Pap... strickly neutral. First fellow that comes along...Yankee, Confederate or just plain ol' Indian...I'm goin' to marry!"

"In that case, girl, it'll probably be just plain Indian then," the old man said matter-of-factly. "For you'll find no white natives on the Golden

Chapter 1: The Coles

Range."

"Thirty years ago, there wasn't a white man from Leavenworth to Chihuahua except Kearney's men. An' never a white woman except the wives of some of the Mormon Battalion...an' they didn't stop long enough to raise any children. Went on up into California to help Fremont, an' then back to Utah an' their own people. Nope… all the whites you will ever see will be some of your own kind, born here in the years to come."

"Makes no difference," Jenny replied, undaunted. "I mean to stay right here the rest of my life! Even if I don't find some prairie boy to marry me. See that draw?" …Pointing. "Off yonder where it comes through the divide? Must be a good ten miles. That's where me an' my man are goin' to homestead... if an' when I get a man. An' he'd, better like it there... 'cause that's where we're goin' to stay."

Following her pointing finger, Pap shook his head. "Draw? That's no draw. That must be where the trail cuts through the divide between the Pawnee an' the Walnut. Old man Harvey was tellin' me last night we could see it from here once we got out of the Walnut bottoms.

"It's the trail from Hays to Dodge. An' Dodge, as you know, is over on the river. Place is gettin' to be quite a town nowadays, they say...what with them Texans trailin' their longhorns up this way. They used to drive through this country to Ellsworth and Abeline. Now they're stoppin' at Dodge. That's why we've not seen any more of them than we have here on the Range."

"Anyway," persisted Jenny. "That's where I'm goin' to build my homestead. Way off yonder where I can see all over the country. You can stay here if you've a mind to."

"Sure like to hear you talk that way, girl," the old man smiled. "That's the spirit it takes in a new country like this." He turned abruptly to

Chapter 1: The Coles

his sons.

"You all might just as well take the same attitude. Because as soon as you're grown, I expect you to take land right around here, too. John and I have papers on these two quarters here in this swale that heads up toward the divide. Before too long, there'll be a family on every quarter section on this prairie! Only thing that grieves me is that I didn't stop here thirty years ago an' build me a fort. Could have had enough cattle now to make you all rich."

"Pap," said Gilbert, one of the younger boys. "Was that cottonwood we passed over the brow of the hill there when you an' Mr. Kearney an' the soldiers passed this way?"

"Yep, son," Pap said. "The General an' me stopped right under that tree there on the ridge an' waited for the others to cross the old Indian ford on the creek back there. Look close an' I expect you'll still find the letters F.C. cut in the bark. I put them there that mornin'. An' I told the General I was comin' back some day an' settle on this land. That tree was the only landmark I had to guide me back."

"Sure was a long time ago," mused the boy. "Still, I bet there are trees down along the creek lots older than that one."

"Sure, boy," agreed Pap. "Lots older. I expect there are trees down there that were older than that one when the Spaniard, Coronado, passed this way over three hundred years ago. Just as soon as we get a house built you an' me will go down there and cut us a ridgepole. Then you can count the rings on the stump an' tell how old the tree really was. Trees grow one ring a year for every year of their life. The big rings show when the met years were; the small rings tell the dry ones. That ought to be fun, don't you think, Gilbert?"

"Oh, yes Pap! An' I can take my musket along an' maybe get us a

Chapter 1: The Coles

rabbit for dinner. Or maybe some quails. Cass said when we crossed the creek, he saw plenty of rabbit signs. An' I know I heard a Bob White callin'!"

"That old musket is going to get you down one of these days, Gil, if you don't watch your step," warned Jake, the next oldest of the boys. "You got to mind how you load her up. She ain't no Gatlin gun. Old Betsy is some sort of a Yankee lady, 'en not to be fooled with. Why yesterday I noticed that jackrabbit you was a shootin' at a scratchin' his ears after he got out of range! You sure must peppered him some. One of these days you're goin' to murder one of them fellows. Then what you goin' to do?"

"You know, Gil, I heard Pap say once that if you wanted to catch a bird all you had to do was put a little salt on his tail. Then you could catch him easy. Why don't you try that on a rabbit one of these days? You might even load old Betsy up with salt. An' then if you didn't kill the rabbit you would at least have salted him so's he would keep 'til you did get him!"

Laughter rippled through the group...the slow, easy laughter of those who understood one another and feared no permanent hurt from a little good natured joshing.

"You can laugh all you are a mind to," Gil said stubbornly, "but I just won't bump the rub!"

<u>Bump the rub</u> was Gilbert's own special saying, and one which none of us ever quite understood. However, he always used the expression to indicate he would not give up something he started until he had accomplished it.

"You fellows think you are so darned smart. You blame old Betsy every time I don't get a rabbit I shoot at. Ain't the gun; it's me. An' I'll have you to understand Betsy ain't no damned Yankee lady either. She's plum Rebel all the way through. Didn't Pap get her at Harper's Ferry where they

Chapter 1: The Coles

hung John Brown on a sour apple tree? He sure did! After he done killed about a dozen Yankees or more with one shot from her! 'En she ain't no bitch either, Betsy ain't, an' I'll have you know that, too! You think I didn't hear you call her that the other day, Mister Jakey, when she kicked you over? Well, I did! An' you didn't get your rabbit either, an' I'm a goin' to tell Ma on you besides if you don't stop cussin like that! Betsy is a plum good old gun! You hear?"

Once you got Gil riled up, there was nothing to do but let him unwind himself. Knowing that, the family sat, smiling, until he finished. Then feeling that perhaps the kidding had gone far enough, John said quietly:

"Why don't you let me load her up for you once, Gil? You're too savin' with your powder. A big army gun like Betsy needs a real man-sized load to do her stuff. Bring her here, boy, an' we'll show Mister Jakey just what a real honest-to-goodness hunter you are. If Pap could get a dozen Yankees at one shot with her, you ought to be able to get a rabbit now and then. Hey, look...there's a big old jack now, settin' behind that weed across the draw. Bet a dollar when we get Betsy loaded up like a Rebel gun should be, you can knock him hell-west-for-crooked from here an' give nobody any odds!

Gil hauled forth the gun and John proceeded to put a real, Man-sized load down her muzzle, ramming the powder home and tamping it down good and tight.

'Now, sonny...' He handed the gun to the boy. "Hold her hard against your shoulder. Then put her right on that jackrabbit's tail an' let him have it!"

Pleased by so much attention, Gil brought the gun hard against his shoulder and fired. Result: the jackrabbit was knocked head over heels from behind the thistle, and the boy was knocked as far in the opposite

Chapter 1: The Coles

direction. His nose bleeding and with tears streaming from his eyes, Gil struggled to his feet. Seeing the rabbit kicking about in its death struggle, he let out a small war whoop of triumph.

"I got him! I got him! See, Pa? See, Ma? Oh, boy, I sure got him that time!'

Leaving the still smoking gun lying in the grass, he ran across the little draw to the big prairie jack and hauled it proudly back to camp.

"Won't have to salt this one's tail, Jakey boy!" he jeered. I guess you fellows will find out one of these days I don't have to bump the rub nohow...not just because you say so!"

Picking up the gun, he walked over to his older brother. "Load her up again, will you John? She sure is some Yankee smasher, old Betsy!"

"What's the matter with your nose, Gil?" Jake said, still teasing the boy. "Looks like old Betsy got rough with you. You sure she's a Rebel gun, the way she kicks at Rebels?"

"I ain't no Rebel, you derned Missouri Puke!" Gil said arrogantly. "I'm a Kansas Red Leg, just new on the Golden Range. Came here with Pap... an' Mr. General Kearney, too... to kill the jackrabbits so's there will be more room for Texas longhorns and other natives. And (looking at Jenny) I mean to stay here. An' I won't bump the rub, never!"

The old man had stood silently watching the scene, his keen eyes missing nothing, his mind absorbing and evaluating the character-words-actions of his boys. Now a pleased smile lit up his face at Gil's words.

"Bravo, boy!" he said. "Clea, get Gil a pan of water and help him get that rabbit blood off his face. An' clean his shirt off while you're at it. Fellow that goes out an' gets game like he does can't help getting a little blood on him. Sure wish the General could have seen that shot. He'd probably have made Gil a Major, first off!"

Chapter 1: The Coles

There was pride in his voice as he spoke...the strong, fierce pride of a man well satisfied with his family. And with life.

These were my people, these hardy pioneers, and I could have asked for none better. They suit me well, these people of the Golden Range. They and their neighbors came from the far places of the world. A great people, a good people, with the majesty and spirit of kings among them and no place in their hearts for tyranny. Happily, I lived in their castles and slept in their courts and found no bigot among them.

2. Pap

If Pap Cole ever had an enemy it was certainly not while living on the Golden Range. Though many of his neighbors had a very wholesome respect for him and the cane he carried, they also considered him a friend...and one to be trusted in any emergency. Yankee and Reb alike... and the lines were pretty well drawn in those early days... considered my grandfather one to whom they could turn in time of distress.

An austere man, he generally kept his own council, with the possible exception of his wife, Susan, and my father, John, in the later years of his life. The boys and girls of the family always addressed him as Pap. We of the second generation always called him <u>Grandpap.</u> His wife and neighbors spoke to and of him as Mr. Cole.

Even old Hank Tenny, the most rabid Yankee who ever came out of York State, always remembered to put the Mr. before Pap's name when writing or speaking. Old Hank was Township Trustee for many years and, in this capacity, once had occasion to help Pap secure a Federal pension as a Mexican war veteran. The Cole clan never thought much of old Hank because of his peppery, overbearing nature, but Grandpap always insisted they treat him with the respect his office entitled him to.

Later, when Grandpap passed on, the clan, pulling together, ousted Tenny from his throne and put a younger and, they supposed, a better man in his place. This ousting created quite a furor in the neighborhood and was the means by which the Cole clan established itself as a 'to be reckoned with' political power on the Golden Range. Learning from this event the power of the minority, my father quickly organized the Cole following into a very potent force in the new county of Ness. In this manner, he was always able to swing the elections in whatever direction was to his advantage.

Chapter 2: Pap

Already well past middle life, Pap (Grandpap, to me) was quite an old man when I can first begin to remember him. My earliest memory is of an old grey-haired man, sitting on the shady side of the house, looking, as I imagined, out over the eastern hills toward the blue valley of the Shenandoah he so often told me-about. Never once did I hear him express a desire to return to that country. Instead, he always swore the Golden Range was the best country on earth and constantly admonished the boys to lay hold of as much of it as they could.

'This is the New America," he would say. "New in every way, this land." And he would wave his cane over the wide sweep of prairie land reaching out to the divide on the south, or up and down the timber land along the creek bottom east and west.

How pleased he was when any of the boys became old enough to take up a homestead or tree claim! Or when some of the older ones became financially able to take a pre-emption.

Get as much of it as you can," he would say. "It may not be worth very much now, but before you boys are as old as I am it will be selling for as much as eastern land."

Time has proven him right. Land for which my father paid one dollar and twenty-five cents per acre would sell today for one hundred dollars per acre.

None of Pap's children knew much about his early life, nor did I ever hear them say a great deal about the Virginia plantation where several of them were born. Only my father seemed to remember very much of those days, and even his recollections were those of a small boy.

One incident which Father never forgot was a fox chase in which Pap and some of his landed friends took part. Being refused permission to go along, Father and one of the colored boys of his own age had to stay at

Chapter 2: Pap

home and plant some herring fish alongside the newly growing corn as fertilizer. The chase, in progress most of the afternoon, ended, incredibly, when the hounds captured the fox not fifty yards from the corn row where the boys were working! For several days, the two strutted around, boasting of how they had been in on the kill. Pap later gave John the fox's tail as a trophy of the chase.

Being the oldest of the grandchildren who lived near Pap, suppose he told me more of his early life than any other one person. From the time I was old enough to hold on to the back of a saddle, I was out with the cattle, riding either with Pap or Jim. Or, occasionally, behind Effie Lee...a situation which I thoroughly detested. Except for Ma and my mother, Jim always tried to make me despise any female member of the family...especially Effie. I liked Effie Lee all right, but I really detested the corset she wore. The darned thing didn't allow for much of a hand hold when the horse broke into a gallop! Also, I much preferred the smell of Horseshoe chewing tobacco associated with Pap and Jim to some of the condiments Effie Lee applied to her person.

Thus it was while riding behind Pap in the long, drowsy, summer days that he told me what little of his early life any of us ever knew.

Pap was the youngest of three boys born to Jacob Cole. Although there were several girls in the Jacob Cole family, I never heard Pap mention any of them except my great aunt, Fanny. He seemed to have a great affection for Aunt Fanny, mentioning her several times in my hearing.

Aunt Fanny married a man by the name of Woods, who later came west to Missouri. Both he and Aunt Fanny died there, leaving two or three children by the marriage. Their son, William, came to the Golden Range country some time after the Coles and homesteaded near the Cole layout. Billy Woods and his wife, Victoria, had five or six girls and one boy,

Chapter 2: Pap

Clyde. Sometimes, these second cousins of mine would add a little to the family history, but not much. Billy was a very taciturn man and Cousin Vic was not too proud of her husband's connections.

Jacob Cole first settled in the Shenandoah Valley in early colonial times, coming to this country from northern Scotland... according to my Grandmother. Grandmother was a Gentry, her people also coming from the north of Scotland about the same time. In fact, she mentioned that the Cole and Gentry families were neighbors there before comin, to America. Here, Jacob Cole had his choice of Virginia land, even as his son, Fayette, had his choice of Golden Range land when first entering the country. A proverb of the Valley in reference to anything unduly long for its width was like Cole's land... 'all long and no wide'. This because he had selected his land up and down the creek bottom because of its fertility and accessibility.

Pap seldom mentioned his oldest brother, Newton; Phillip, the next youngest, was his favorite. But sometime quite early in the history of this country... possibly during the troublous days of Aaron Burr... my Uncle Newt had occasion to go to New Orleans. He was never heard from again. Uncle Phillip, seeking his lost brother, went, too, into the bayou country. And, like Newt, he was never heard from again.

Being the only man left in the family, Pap carried on for some time. But when the Mexican War broke out, he enlisted in the Army and, too, went into that wild, new land...hoping to learn something of his lost brothers.

We of the Cole clan used to suspect that Pap had actually found out more about his elusive brothers than he cared to disclose. However that may be, he came back to the plantation after the war and, assuming ownership of the land and slaves, carried on until the Civil War put an end to it all.

Chapter 2: Pap

Pap's marriage to my Grandmother was one more of convenience than of love. With the Cole and Gentry families living so close to one another, it was virtually impossible to keep the young Negroes belonging to the two families from falling in love across the boundary lines. After this had gone on for some time, ownership of the resulting children from these unions became a difficult problem. To rectify the situation, the two families proposed the marriage of Susan Gentry and my Grandfather. By this arrangement, the Gentry Negroes became Cole Negroes and life on the plantations went on much as usual.

From the end of the Mexican War to the end of the Civil War, Pap's life on the plantation was much that of the average Virginia gentleman of the times. He never told me much about that period, but, with my aunts and uncles coming on the scene by this time, much of it has been handed down from that source.

Coming west after the Civil War, Pap settled in western Missouri for about eleven years. Then a haunting memory of the Kansas prairies, seen almost thirty years before, started him moving again in search of that lost paradise. The result was, of course, the ranch on the Walnut Creek in the Golden Range country.

Pap never seemed so happy as when he could gather his children and grandchildren about him for a family reunion. The one big day of the year was Christmas. Then we all went home to Pap's for a full twenty-four hours of feasting and good times.

Everybody for miles around managed to drop in at the Coles on Christmas Day... and all were welcome. As many as three hundred people have eaten Christmas dinner at Pap's. No one ever went away hungry, and many carried home enough food to last through the following week.

When a professional baker moved into the country one summer, Pap hired him to bake the cakes for the following Christmas. Twenty-four

Chapter 2: Pap

of them, the baker turned out all huge affairs. But the piece de resistance was a giant baked in Grandmother's wash tub... and coated all over with candy and fancy frosting!

At these 'come one come all' reunions old feuds were forgotten. An' many a prairie boy and girl owe their existence to love affairs which grew out of these neighborly get-togethers.

Pap's word was as good as his bond. What he said he would do he did...never quibbling nor trying to avoid an unpleasant situation in which he may have gotten himself. Although he generally weighed any circumstance which arose pretty thoroughly, once he committed himself, his follow up along those lines could be pretty well depended upon. Naturally, there were those who took advantage of his integrity. From time to time, members of the clan managed to selfishly usurp the limited privileges granted to the large Cole following.

For instance, the Federal government's quarterly payment of eight dollars a month for Pap's Mexican War service was no great amount of cash. Especially when it must be distributed impartially among so many growing boys and girls. On occasion, Pap forgot just how little it really was. Once he promised Jim two dollars from his next check for a pair of wooden stirrups like Andy Wolf's. Jim didn't particularly need the stirrups, but since Pap had promised, Jim held him to it. Nor did Effie Lee's tirading about the matter result in anything more than wasted breath. Pap was adamant. Certainly Effie Lee needed a new calico much more than Jim needed the stirrups... but Jim got the stirrups.

Another time, when young John broke the code, Grandma cut herself a keen willow switch and called him on the carpet. Pap, always in sympathy with his eldest son, insisted he become bondsman and receive the punishment instead of the boy. Her anger already somewhat abated, Grandma accepted the substitute. But other things coming up just then,

Chapter 2: Pap

she laid aside her switch and went about her affairs. Apparently, she forgot all about the matter. But two or three days later, when Pap was stooped over pulling some weeds in the garden, a keen willow switch came whistling down across his posterior!

Snapping erect, Pap tried to grab the supple willow, at the same time exclaiming, "Hey, Susan, what on earth are you doing anyway?"

"Just giving you John's licking," she said calmly. "Come on... bend over, Mister Cole!"

"Oh," Pap said. "I clean forgot about it."

Dutifully, he turned his back and bent over.

Grandma laid it on, I am told, until her conscience would allow no more. Then throwing the frayed willow away, she went into the house.

Such a man was Pap, and such was his word.

All that summer, the cyclones had been spotting down over the prairies almost every night. My cousin, Clee Whipple, Grandma and myself spent every night in the dugout cellar in the bank of the draw. Pap slept in the nice soft bed in the upstairs room of the new frame ranch house. The mornings were wonderful after the drenchings of the night before. But we were always groggy from the dampness of the leaky cellar and the cramped quarters on the dirt floor.

Each morning, Pap emerged fresh as a daisy from the house after a good night's sleep. When questioned about his indifference to the storms, he insisted he would just as soon go to heaven on a cyclone as any other way.

Exasperated, Grandma retorted: "It light be all right, Mister Cole, if you were going that way. But it would be an awful drop if, by chance, you were headed in the other direction!"

Chapter 2: Pap

Pap still continued to sleep in the house.

He was not one to change his ways, even when threatened by a cyclone trip to Hell!

The Coles were mostly a religious people, however uncivilized some of them might seem to be, but none of us knew if Pap had ever belonged to a church. Never were any of us certain of this while living on the Golden Range. However, I have known him to divide his eight dollar a month pension with some destitute preacher's family. And he would always kneel with them in prayer when they came to visit with him in his home.

When asked on his deathbed concerning his future expectations, he said simply,

"I have lived; I am not afraid to die."

A phlegm gathering in his throat just before death, he asked my father to remove it, then said banteringly:

"I always thought I would be a rich man some day. Now, look! I'm so rich I can't even spit off my own property!"

And he died.

The American Legion Post in our home town of Bazine, near the old Cole ranch, bears the name <u>Olin Cole Post</u> named for one of Pap's great grandsons who lost his life on the Anzio beach head in World War II. On Decoration Day, the Stars and Stripes wave over three graves... Pap's, his grandson's and his great grandson's.

A Mexican War veteran...a World War I veteran... a World War II veteran.

The Coles were never cowards.

3. Some Sons-in-Law

"The Devil owed old man Cole a grudge and paid him off in sons-in-law!"

Such was neighbor Mooney's opinion of certain of my uncles with whom he had had a bit of misunderstanding.

Seymour Mooney was from Vermont, with all of a Yankee's rigidity of opinion, and in no manner on speaking terms with the Devil. So how he knew all this was a mystery. Nor did it ever enter my boyish mind to question his terse statement. We all respected Seymour Mooney too much to question anything he might say.

Nonetheless, I used to often wonder just what the 'grudge' might have been. And why the Devil had chosen such a splendid medium of exchange to fulfill his obligation.

Pap Cole seemed not in the least worried about the matter, accepting his sons-in-law with a certain equanimity which suggested he considered the debt well discharged. Always they had a place in his home and, seemingly, in his affections, equal to that of the daughter responsible for their position. Sons they were to him, and as sons they were treated, even though four of the five came from north of the Mason-Dixon line.

Pap Cole never let the war come between him and a neighbor, much less those who had chosen to become a part of his household. Nor did he ever fight another battle after he laid down his musket at Appomattox. Yet his word was law, among those of his family and his will very much considered, even though he seldom allowed himself the luxury of an argument. It was always 'thus and so' with him, and none of us...even the sons-in law...ever thought to question a thing Pap said.

The day after he reached the Golden Range, Pap first met one of

Chapter 3: Some Sons-in-Law

these future-sons-in-law.

They arrived on the twenty-sixth of October. The following day, being Sunday, the little company took a much needed rest.

Unloading the two wagons, they turned one of the wagon boxes upside down for a table. The beds were spread about on the soft brown prairie grass in the fervent hope that there would be no rain. Not for a few days at least. (I never did hear whether or not it rained before Pap roofed the dugout he had secured along with the relinquishment on the quarter section he had chosen.)

As in the old life... 'beyond the wide Missouri'... the women made a little extra effort for this first Sunday dinner in this new country. I am told that Grandma Cole even went so far as to open one of her few cans of peach preserves for the occasion.

The fourteen of them had just seated themselves around the overturned wagon box when two strangers were seen approaching from over the western hills. They were on foot, a mode of travel not much used on the big prairies in those days, it being considered both dangerous as well as exceedingly uncomfortable. Especially if one had no outfit for protection. These two obviously had nothing save the clothes on their backs.

"Be they Indians, do you think, Pap?"

As one, the group turned to the old man who had risen and now stepped forward to greet the two strangers.

"Bet a dollar they be natives," whispered the boy, Gilbert, to his sister, Jenny. "Just the same, maybe I better get ole Betsy. They maybe could be Injuns come all the way from Chihuahua to gobble up the Golden Range."

Slipping under the wagon, he brought the old gun out and laid it

Chapter 3: Some Sons-in-Law

carefully alongside his place at the table.

Of the two strangers, one was an old man, plainly dressed and wearing rough cow-hide boots. The other, a boy whose age might have been anywhere from sixteen to twenty, presented in incongruous figure. Both women and men stared at him with open curiosity.

He wore a one piece suit of what might once have been a pair of denim overalls. Now they boasted no buttons and only one suspender, drawn diagonally across his right shoulder from a nail pushed through the band several inches past center on the left side and brought to a like anchorage in the back. The left leg, very badly frayed, came about halfway from belt to knee; the right just to the knee.

That was all.

No hat, no shirt, no vest, no shoes.

His face and the exposed parts of his lanky body were coated a beautiful prairie tan, and a shock of uncut hair reached nearly to his shoulders.

"There's your native Jenny!" snickered Gilbert. "Better homestead him right away and scoot off yonder on the divide. 'Cause he's sure enough native. Bet a dollar you'll never find another just like him... not even if you looked all over the Golden Range for thirty years."

"Oh, do be still, Gil!" whispered Jenny. "Can't you see Pa's done gone and invited them to dinner!"

Soon the strangers were seated at the wagon box table, wolfing the food set down before them.

Many years later I asked my Mother how they spent that first Sunday afternoon on the prairies.

"Well, there just wasn't much to do," he said. "But some of the

Chapter 3: Some Sons-in-Law

boys proposed we go for a walk across the draw to some rocky flats there. We had great fun picking up the pretty rocks that were scattered all over the place. Somehow, Jenny and the strange boy got paired off together and managed to have a great time getting acquainted."

Two years later, Jenny and Ira Whipple enjoyed the distinction of being the first couple to be married in the newly organized county.

Some years later, when I was born on the Golden Range, no name seemed so well suited for me as that of this stranger who had made himself so much one of the family. Becoming his namesake, he always seemed to mean more to me than any of my other uncles.

Having secured her 'native", Jenny was delighted to find that he had already homesteaded a quarter section of land far up on the divide...in the exact spot she had first pointed out as her choice of the Golden Range country.

The old Dodge trail went right across the corner of the homestead. In those days when I first began to remember events, my cousins, the Whipples... of whom there were eight born on the place... used to make their play-houses in the ruts where ox wagons had once rumbled.

It was always a great day for we younger ones when we were taken to Jenny's and Uncle Ira's for a visit. We were all loaded into the big wagon... grandad, grandma, father, mother, my brothers and sisters, and those of the aunts and uncles yet at home... and away we would go to spend the week-end at the Whipples.

Their dugout was not very big, at first... consisting only of two rooms. However, there always seemed to be plenty of room for everybody present. I can well remember awakening in the morning when there was not a single foot of room on the dirt floor that was not occupied by a bed and sleepers.

Chapter 3: Some Sons-in-Law

Often, along with the Coles, came the Styments, the Glaspeys or some of the Shabens or Reeds... and, frequently, they all came together. My uncle kept a social board in those days and every traveller was more than welcome.

Almost, I can hear him yet, calling in his deep voice to Aunt Jenny: "Hey, Nade! A nickname for his wife. "Nade, shake a foot there and get these kids something to eat! Can't you see they're dern near starved!"

And starved we generally were, what with all the new world around us, and the million things for youths like us to be doing. No day was ever long enough. And the nights might have been eternities so soundly did we sleep through them. Yet Uncle Ira's booming voice always brought us out of it and started us on another round of adventure.

Yes, the Whipples were a wonderful people, and I have always been proud they were kin of mine. What an honor to have been named after such a-grand old man as my Uncle Ira!

In later life, my Aunt Jenny became affiliated with the Mormon Church, but I don't recall whether or not Uncle Ira ever joined up. It was always a saying of his... when anything was ever said about going to Heaven, or the 'hereafter'... that he was going in on Nade's pinnin blanket. Just what a pinnin blanket was remained a mystery, for I never gained the courage to inquire.

However he traveled, I'm sure he got there. Like Jim Bludso in the poem: "At Judgement, I'd take my chances with him, longside of some pious gentlemen who wouldn't have shook hands with him."

For fifty years, the Whipples lived on the homestead on the divide, adding many a quarter section to that first holding. Both died with it still in their names. Uncle Ira went first... much like he came to the Golden Range...in a careless, big hearted way, mourned by every one whom he

Chapter 3: Some Sons-in-Law

had ever met. All his earthly possessions, he left to Jenny, the girl who, that first Sunday, went hunting with him for pretty rocks across the draw.

4. "I won't bump the rub!"

"Gilbert! You come here this very minute! Take a look at them boot straps of yours! A hangin' down like the lop ears of old Uncle Billy Hayes' mule!"

"I swear, boy, I don't know what to do about you. Can't you get them boots on without pullin' the ears off? I have a mind to have your Pa give you a good cow-hidin' for bein' so ever-olastin' sloppy. Why, you look as run down as that Whipple kid who was here yesterday with old man Hurd. Suppose you think he was a sight to draw to!"

"Now you get on over there where John's fixin' them harness an' have him put a good big copper rivet on them straps. An' mind you, ill catch 'em floppin' again, I'll cut 'em both off slick to the boots! Then what will you do? Step lively now...if you want to go with Pap an' the boys after that new ridge pole!"

This was Grandma Cole... 'Ma' as everybody called her... taking Gil to task for having pulled the straps loose from the copper toed boots Pap had bought him just before leaving Missouri.

Sullenly, Gil started to move away. As he did so Effie Lee sidled up to Ma.

"Ma, I seed Gil deliberately pull them straps loose this very day," she said. "Not ten minutes after Pa fixed 'em for him! An' he was cussin' somethin' awful, too, while he was doin' it."

"That's a lie Ma!" Gil yelled. "Just as sure as Eff's a long horn heifer what's runnin' wild out of Texas! 'n if she don't cut it out pretty soon... a lyin' about me... me and Mr. General Kearney's a goin' to round her up an' trail her into Dodge an' sell her to the Mormon Battalion! 'n they'll take her right back to their people in Utah where she'll die plum

Chapter 4: "I won't bump the rub!"

dead with the dysentery and typhoid! Guess she'll be plenty sorry then. Only it'll be too late!"

"You Gilbert!" exclaimed Ma Cole. "You come right here this very minute! The very idea of you talkin' like that.

"Here Effie Lee! Hand me a piece of that soap over there. I'll wash some of that nasty talk out of his dirty mouth!"

"There now!" Suiting the action to the word. "Get on over there an' get them boots fixed up. An' after this be a little more careful about boastin' about what you an' that stinkin' Yankee General's goin' to do!"

"Well, I just won't bump the rub!" Gil howled, spitting and frothing at the mouth and looking daggers at his sister. As he started toward his older brother, he threw a last defiant blast over his shoulder.

"Just you wait! One of these days when I get strong enough, 'n get a pair of boot straps stout enough to lift me, I'll come sailin' around up in the air an' I'll drop right plum square down on Eff's frizzy noggin' 'n I'll knock every dern bit of the lie right kerslap out of her! Then you'll all be sorry you done hurt my feelings like you have. A callin' Mr. General Kearney a damn Yankee, when everybody knows he's a plum Christian gentleman, same as me an' Pap."

"You, Gilbert!" Ma Cole picked up the soap and started toward the boy. "You're just gettin' too smart for your britches aroun' here!"

But Gil had already sought refuge behind his older brother, John, who had been an interested bystander.

Tell me, Gil," John said. "Just what is the matter with them boot straps anyway? Can't understand myself why you have to pull 'em off every time you put your boots on. I don't treat mine that way, an' I'm a lot bigger'n you."

Chapter 4: "I won't bump the rub!"

For a moment, the boy regarded him speculatively. "Bout how much do you weigh, John?"

"Oh, about a hundred and forty-five pounds, I imagine," his brother replied. "Why?"

"I was just wonderin'." Still wiping the soapsuds from his mouth, Gil looked disgustedly toward camp, where his mother and sister were washing dishes. Then he switched back to his brother.

"How many pounds you think you could lift, John, if you tried your very best?"

John shrugged. "Probably two hundred and fifty, maybe three hundred pounds. Now, stop askin' questions. Here are your boots. Be a little more careful next time you put 'em on. Especially if you're feelin' a little extra strong."

"All right," Gil agreed. Then, persistently: "How much you think I weigh?"

John pursed his lips a moment. "Well...I expect you weigh all of fifty pounds by this time. You sure been shootin' right up there since we came to the Golden Range."

Gil's face lighted. "Bout how much you think I could lift right now if I had a good holt on it"

"You ought to be able to lift almost a hundred pounds by now," his brother replied. "Why don't you try that sack of meal over there. It's a fifty pounder. About as big as you are anyway. A little. hard to get hold of maybe. But if you can lift that, I bet -you could lift a hundred if it had handles on it."

Without further comment, Gil gathered onto the fifty pound sack of meal. With some little difficulty, he managed to carry it several yards

Chapter 4: "I won't bump the rub!"

before setting it down.

"I told you I could do it!" he exclaimed, his face flushed with triumph. "Now you can bet I won't bump the rub! You can just bet I won't!"

And with a boot strap in each hand, he walked off over the little hill behind the rock walls of the unfinished house.

That afternoon, the ridge pole was cut and brought from the creek almost two miles away. Since it was, quite an undertaking most of the men and boys took part, Gil along with them.

A long, straight red elm was selected for the log. After it was cut and trimmed of its branches, it was worked onto the running gears of the wagon. To accommodate It, the wagon had to be coupled out as long as the reach would permit.

After the pole was loaded, the remainder of the tree was piled on as well.

Although I am not sure, I think I have heard my mother say that Grandpap Cole gave two dollars and fifty cents for the tree. Once the pole was in place on the stone walls of the house, the branches were used for rafters. On top of these branches were placed a quantity of prairie grass and sunflowers. Several loads of dirt from the nearby hill were then pressed into shape... and, lo, my people had a roof over their heads!

Going home that night, the crowd of men and boys rode perched about on the branches of the tree, having fun and making a picnic of the affair.

It was while holding Gil in his place among the branches that John happened to see the boy's boots. The boot straps which he had so recently fastened with copper rivets were again torn loose.

Chapter 4: "I won't bump the rub!"

"Holy Moses, Gil," he exclaimed. "How in thunder did you pull them ears off your boots again? Pap, I just fixed them straps this mornin'. Now, take a look at 'em! Gil, what in the world did you have your boots off for this afternoon anyway?"

"I didn't have 'em off, John; honest." Gil began to cry. "But I just won't bump the rub! Derned if I will! You know blamed well I can lift more than fifty pounds. You see'd me do it this mornin'. Anyways, you didn't more than half fix them straps with your old copper rivets!"

At this point, Jake spoke up and solved the mystery of Gil's strange behavior. He had seen Gil down by the creek bank while the others were busy with the tree.

"The derned little idiot was pullin his guts out, tryin' to lift himself by his boot straps! He got mad as the devil 'cause I told him it couldn't be done. Swore I was crazy... 'cause he didn't weigh no more than fifty pounds. And he'd lifted more than that this mornin'. Well, he kept on tryin' until them boot straps busted again. Then he throwed mud all over me for laughin' at him. I told him he was sure goin't to bump the rub this time."

"Why, you derned Missouri Puke," sobbed the boy. "I just won't bump the rub an' that's that nohow!"

Later, Grandpap Cole consoled the boy... and secretly fixed the boot straps again before Ma could see them.

Several days later, a bright November day, Effie Lee came in and reported to Ma in scandalized tones:

"That Gil's down there in the bottom of the draw just natcherly cussin' a blue streak. And with nothin' whatever to cuss at or about! Just a cussin' cause he can and wants to.

"I see'd him just now, a runnin' up an' down the draw like a little devil. An' every time he went so far one way, he would stop and clap his

Chapter 4: "I won't bump the rub!"

hands and laugh an' say somethin' to his self... just like he was mighty tickled about somethin'. But when he ran the other way, he would get mad an' cuss an' cry like nobody's business. Guess the little goose has gone plum crazy!'

"You get on back there," ordered Ma. "an' try and find out what it's all about. That sun yesterday was plenty hot. An' I noticed he was off about the same place, a runnin' up an' down the draw. But I didn't hear him a cussin' or a cryin'."

She paused and fixed Effie Lee with a suspicious eye. "Sometimes, girl, I think you like to torment Gil... just because he be a mite stubborn like an' set in his ways. Now, go on. An' don't say nothin' to make him mad. Just bring him up here in the shade of the wagon to cool off a bit. He sure beats any kid I ever saw to get outlandish notions about what he can or can't do!"

"Ifn't he was my kid," said Effie Lee, "know what I'd do for him? I'd get me one of them limbs off that ridge pole there, an' I'd just naturally thrash the daylights plum out'n the little devil! I'd bump his rub once'd he never would forget!"

"You an' Pap sure do humor him somethin' frightful. Why, that little stinker's got a notion he's greater than God Almighty Hisself! A tryin' to lift himself by his boot straps, and such things what there ain't no sense to whatever. Won't bump the rub, huh! If I had my way with him, he'd bump his rub alright!"

"Now that'll do, Effie Lee," Ma said tartly. "You get on down there and get that little rascal...'fore he runs himself clear to death. There he goes again! Just a tearin' into it like a race horse! Whatever in the world he thinks he's a doin' is beyond me... a runnin' like a mad dog in the summer time!"

Chapter 4: "I won't bump the rub!"

"That's one of his cussin' streaks," Effie Lee volunteered. "See him poundin' the ground in front of him... just like he was fightin' his shadow? The stinkin' little dummy! If I go down there, I'm goin' to drag him up here somethin' awful!"

"You be careful how you talk to Gil," Ma warned. "He ain't got much use for you girls nohow."

It took Effie Lee quite a while to get the boy started toward the house. And only then by making him so mad he tried to catch her; she running that way and he following.

Approaching her mother, she shouted: "The little goose was a tryin' to run down his own shadow! Just look how dirty and sweaty he is. A runnin' his silly head off an' gettin' nothin' out of it but his bump rubbed! Oh...!" The exasperated girl went off into a fit of gleeful laughter.

Gil glared at her, his perspiring face cherry red. "Nothin' but a long horned heifer!" he yelled. "A dern long horned heifer, straight out of Texas! Laugh, you ijit! But I'm tellin' you... I won't 'bump the rub, never! Not for all the longhorns this side of Chihuahua! If I can beat that blamed shadow half the time, the way I'm doin', sooner or later I'll get fast enough to beat it all the time! Anyway, I'm goin' to keep on tryin' 'til I do. An' I just won't bump the rub!"

5. Concerning the Autumn

There was something so unutterably lonely about the prairies in the Autumn time, it made one wish to go away forever into some other land. Where that land might be seemed to make but little difference just so one escaped the terrible, soul-crushing loneliness on every side.

Death seemed all about us. Not death as we had aver known it, but an everlasting, hopeless death. A. death with no promise of a resurrection, no hope of a hereafter, no looking beyond the veil. An everlasting, hopeless death, reaching out and away forever. An end, as though one had come to the edge of the Universe, with never another step to be taken. Infinitesimally infinite...innumerable quantity... a thorough death. A death with never a thought of Life again, with never a hope of Life again as if in this, all things that ever were had come to an end...and there be no need to save or think of plan forever more.

So great a pain of loneliness seized upon one in this supreme hour that the tears started and the breath was broken and the heart almost ceased to beat. A pain not as any other pain, but a pain wherein there was no hope for relief, nor even desire for relief. A pain that was not, that could never be, that never existed and yet was more terribly real than one's own life.

I knew myself, my hopes my desires, but I did not know this thing that came in so stealthily on the night wind from the south and that morning gathered up all of mine that ever existed.

Where did they go to, my treasures? I turned on every side, where so lately they had lain, piled in confusion, and I found no one thing that ever I knew, and my heart broke with the unspeakable loneliness of the thrice dead world around me... the prairie in Autumn.

The Creek that but yesterday was a shining ribbon of green and gold stretching away into the unknown west... or east into the land of

Chapter 5: Concerning the Autumn

morning... today was a dead serpent, spent and decaying in an already dead world. The miles and miles of prairie, spotted here and there with flowery fields of paradise... or flecked with magic lakes of mirage... today had turned into a burned out waste, with never again a hope of tomorrow. There was no soothing in the wind that came so mournfully across the brown monotony. And the voice that yesterday, was so vibrant with life and hope, was, today, a dirge of the dead; in a voice of the dead, sing of the dead things to dead things, and I knew that Autumn had come.

The sentinel antelope atop the little hill on the western slope was no living thing. That morning, he frolicked with his fellows in the promise of a new day; at noon, he rested in the shadow of the rock of ages. But then the night came, the Autumn, and, with no hope of another spring time, that evening he was only a statue of clay, shadowed forever in the light of a dead day.

The great flock of crows, coming in so silently to roost in the old elm in the bend of the creek were not living things. Yesterday, they were... cawing just as lustily as the rest of us when they went out into the morning. But now, the autumn had come to them, too, the autumn of the prairies, and they were only ghostly things that died when summer went away on the south wind that morning. They had no voice.

Only that last, far-flung cry on the southern rim, where the divide came up to meet the stars, was of the yesterday. The voice of the wild goose as he fled from the death on every side. Yesterday, he tarried with his fellows in the shallow pools, sporting with fate, but willing to take a, chance that he might garner the fruit of the land. Yet the night saw the last of him and he was gone, and the Autumn came down on every side and that last, lone cry made the loneliness more lonely.

Death of Baldur. End of all things. Autumn on the prairies.

Scarcely was the new roof on the little house in the bank of the

Chapter 5: Concerning the Autumn

draw than the older men must hurry away. Back along the road they had so lately come, seeking such work as might be had in the more settled country.

The corn crop, what there was of it in that year 1878, was considered pretty good. And there had been promise of work for those who cared to go and gather it in. Therefore, Grandpap, my father, John, and all the rest, from Cass up, went away into eastern Kansas to shuck corn.

How my father ever made anything at shucking corn, don't know. Years later, when we had a crop in our part of the state, his efforts along those lines were nothing phenomenal! But then circumstances alter cases sometimes. He had money with which to have his own corn gathered.

In 1878, fifty cents per day, and board, was considered pretty good. Especially so when, as in the case of the Cole family, there were several workers. Since all the wages went into one pot, they did very well. At least, they stayed in the corn country until late in the winter, or until the corn was gathered.

After the men had gone east, the women and children had time to realize that it would be many weeks before their return. Yet money they must have if they were to stay in this new land. So they sat back to wait the long weeks out.

And then it was that the awful loneliness of the prairies in autumn made itself feat.

Of all the hardships these people suffered, it seems to me this loneliness was the most virile. There were no other houses on that wide expanse of prairie to be seen that first winter... and very few neighbors within walking distance of the dugout in the bank of the draw. Fortunately, there were several women and children in the Cole family. This plus the ever presence of necessity, helped.

Chapter 5: Concerning the Autumn

As Grandma was wont to say, "the scratchin' of our wits to keep from starvin' an' freezin' kept time from hangin' too heavy on our hands.'

All this was after winter had set in in earnest. For there is a great difference between winter and autumn on the prairies. Winter is something to grapple with, something tangible and real, and comes with a reality not to be misunderstood. Winter points somewhere, and, once one finds oneself at grips with it, there is no looking back. Only a certain rush and hurrah that leaves one breathless but very much alive... on the threshold of Spring. Autumn is otherwise and, by its very insidiousness, leaves one vanquished even before the fight begins.

Sometimes, the wild cattle grazed nearby, but they were afraid to tarry long. And the antelope stayed on the far ridge lest, as Gil said, lest he take a shot at them with old Betsy.

One day my Mother noticed a bunch of the shy creatures near the bank of the draw, but almost a mile further up. Bored with the eternal loneliness, she took an old revolver of my father's and crawled all but the entire mile in the bottom of the draw... just to get a shot at them. When she, at last, raised up for the shot, the antelope were on the ridge another mile away. They had picked up her scent.

Wild geese were there, too, in countless numbers, but always hurrying by... as if afraid of the desolation below. Sometimes they stopped long enough to drink from the big buffalo wallow on the far side of the claim. Or to gather a cropfull of sunflower seeds from the abundance spread all over the prairies.

One day Cass and Jake managed to slip up on a big bunch of them so occupied, and killed one outright with old Betsy, breaking the wing of another. The crippled one, an old gander, put up such a fight before he was killed that the boys were covered with blood from head to foot. Grandma had a great time repairing their clothes! However, the wild game was a

Chapter 5: Concerning the Autumn

very welcome addition to the meager larder, and made a great story to tell the men folks when they at last came home.

Sometimes they quarreled among themselves, these women of mine, and made faces at one another, and pouted and wouldn't speak and the stranger among them, who was to become my mother, suffered the most I think. For she often went out alone along the rocky hillsides to gather pretty rocks... and to cry and to dream of the old home in Missouri.

But she was brave and fought back at the loneliness of the autumn, and sometimes wrote little verses on scraps of paper and sang songs into the wind, and waited for the day when she would have her own home on her own land. And, withal, she came to love the prairies with a love that has lasted for a hundred and two years.

She is still alive on the Golden Range, the very last of that little company who fought against the desolation of that first autumn.

It was she who told me just the other day, as it were: "After dinner, we went over 'long the rocky flats and picked up pretty rocks."

6. About Some Horses and Their Riders

In that year of 1878, I suppose there were more people on the Golden Range than even my people realized. Certainly I have heard them mention first this one and then that one and some little adventure that befell various others. And, in looking over the written history of the time, it is clear that there was a great rush of settlers all over that part of the land. At best, it must have been a big country, and a lonely one with the settlers very much scattered.

Travel was either by horse or ox team... or on horseback, And a mile was quite a long way if negotiated on foot. Thirty miles was a long day's journey, for a team and wagon if the team be horses. Ten or twelve, if it be oxen.

A man, if he was a good walker, could kill a horse in a day to day endurance test. Somehow, reason has a supremacy over brute strength, even though the brute strength be directed by human reason. In those days, I remember a professional walker, Payson by name, who thought nothing of walking ninety to a hundred miles in a day. He did this many days in a row, something no horse was able to accomplish. In a single day, I have known this man to walk one hundred and fifteen miles! From sunup to sundown! The judges had to change horses quite often while he just walked on from day to day.

Nonetheless, there was many a good horse on the prairie... and many the tales recounted of some special journey or ride made by both man and beast.

An outstanding case was Bob Giton's ride, made in those days when my people first came to the Golden Range country. It seems Giton had located himself a claim somewhere between Dodge and Hayes, and had then gone back to Missouri to find work.

Chapter 6: About Some Horses and Their Riders

Early the next spring, when Giton had been away from his claim almost six months, word got around that a certain party on the Range intended to jump Giton's claim immediately the six months were up. That is, unless Giton was on it by that time.

Now my father had become acquainted with Giton, who was working at a still in the little town of Lone Jack, just before coming to the plains country himself. Therefore, upon hearing this rumor, Father felt that his friend might wish to hold the place. (A homesteader must spend at least one night in six months on the land to prove it up and get a patent from the government.) So, driving into Hayes, he telegraphed Giton at Lone Jack about the situation.

Receiving the message, Giton found himself on the spot. For, by starting at once, he had only three days and nights to make the ride from Lone jack, forty miles east of Kansas City in Jackson County, Missouri to the claim, somewhere in Trego County in western Kansas. Three days to ride a little over three hundred miles... and only one little fantail prairie bronc to do the trick!

Well, the bronc wasn't worth much, at best, and a whole quarter section of prairie land was at stake and it was springtime and the call of Kansas was in the air...

John Henry Shawhan stood in the still-house door early that Monday morning, just as the first rays of the sun were peeking over the tree tops toward the east, and wished Bob Giton bon voyage on his westward journey.

A pint flask of Lone Jack whiskey in his pocket and another alongside the lunch in his saddlebags, a gift from John Henry, a good luck from the still-house crew., and Giton and the fantail were away.

Early the following Thursday morning, the last of the six months

Chapter 6: About Some Horses and Their Riders

being spent, a wagon loaded with household goods turned into the yard of a Kansas soddy.

Behind the soddy, well out of sight, the shadow of what had been the fantail stood on three legs head drooping and eyes closed in slumber. Back of the door in the shadows, an old rifle clutched in his hands, stood Bob Giton.

The wagon rumbled to a stop, and the man on the seat jumped down and began to unhitch the horses.

"Stoppin' for breakfast?" Stepping out into the morning sunlight, the boy brought the old rifle to the ready.

"Well, I'll be damned!," The man froze, staring at the boy in amazement. "How in hell did you get here, Giton?"

"Old Baldy," the boy replied tersely. Then: "You sneakin' son of a bitch! What you startin' to unload that stuff for? Must think you own this place. Well, you don't, you dirty four flusher! An' just as soon as you can get that grub box an' a sack of them oats unloaded, you better hightail it out of here. Before Old Baldy and me ride over to Dodge an' get the U.S. Marshall after you!"

I am told that the man obeyed, not even resenting the boy's harsh words. Before leaving, he even took a good look at the fantail who had ambled around the corner of the soddy.

"Don't give him too many oats at first," he said throwing the sack on the ground. "An' if you had a little whiskey to pour over his food, it might keep him from bloating."

"It's all gone," said the boy. "Gave him the last of it 'bout an hour ago."

Then there is the story of our own Jim Stephens who, during the

Chapter 6: About Some Horses and Their Riders

World's Fair at Chicago, rode for Kansas in the all out cowboy derby... ending up before the race track grandstand.

Just how many entries there were in the race is lost in memory, but I remember with what interest we watched the newspapers for word of the finish. Well, Jim tied with some other cowboy...and then, no one knows quite how, managed to talk the judges into believing he was the better of the two! Since the race was judged not only by the time made per day, but by the condition of both horse and rider...as well as other 'uncertain' factors...there was a good deal of leeway in judging. There, talk went a long ways, and Jim was quite some talker!

It was hinted that Jim carried too much liquor, even for that time, coming as he did from a prohibition state. Of course this was only hearsay...as was the rumor that the judges disqualified him, in a manner, for this. However, being of a frugal mind, it was presumed that he did drink the last of his whiskey just before encountering the judges... rather than contribute to moral delinquency by discarding it in the streets of Chicago.

'Talk' or no, it would be hard even at this late date, to make some of those old Alexander boys think Jim wasn't the best cowboy to ride into Chicago for the great World's Fair...

My uncle Gilbert...he of "I won't bump the rub!" fame... grew up to become one of the noted riders of the plains. In fact, his prowess as a rider and bronc buster spread over several states. Many was the rancher who employed him for no other reason than to break the wild horses that others could not ride.

Probably because of the very persistency of his will, he never allowed a horse to conquer him. Nor did he ever give up until he had

Chapter 6: About Some Horses and Their Riders

mastered the animal in every sense of the word. Just to be able to ride the creature was not his idea of a broken horse. The animal must be tamed and gentled and made to yield his strength and intelligence to the use of his master in whatever line of work he was broken to.

Time seemed not to enter into my uncle's calculation of things. On occasion, I have known him to contract to break a horse for a certain purpose... and then to work with that horse for a year or more. Or until the horse became what the owner expected him to be. All this for no greater sum than five dollar, the contract price for the job!

Uncle Gil seemed able to develop the better points of a horse over his weaker ones. And to bring them into general use in a manner unequaled by any other man following this calling in that time of much horsemanship.

If the occasion arose for the use of a common or mediocre horse in some extraordinary event, Gil could be expected to get the utmost out of him...where other riders would have failed completely.

He was able to quickly size up a horse and in a few hours of handling could pass judgement on whether the animal was good, bad or indifferent. Usually his judgment proved correct. This ability of his was no doubt responsible for the men of our house having so many splendid horses in their remuda.

Vividly I call to mind a little buckskin outlaw my uncle bought from a fellow who deemed the horse almost worthless. And, in truth, the animal seemed to have no stamina, as well as being of a vicious and uncertain disposition.

Gil, being certain there was good in the animal, bought him contrary to my father's advice. He then went about training the brute's better nature with such success that in a few weeks time he was able to run

Chapter 6: About Some Horses and Their Riders

down and kill four coyotes on the horse! And with seemingly little inconvenience to the animal!

How well I remember that day! Mounted on one of the heavier work horses, I was riding with my uncle that morning. We were looking for some stray cattle that had been away from the home range for several days. He was mounted on old Buck, as he now called the little buckskin. As a result of his careful training, Buck bore but little resemblance to the vicious five dollar outlaw he had been only a few weeks before.

Shortly before sun-up, we came suddenly on a pack of four coyotes. Evidently they had breakfasted, possibly on some rancher's chickens, or maybe a jackrabbit... for they were quite lazy. Soon after we discovered them, they went into hiding in the tall grass at the head of a little draw. I remember they sort of scattered up and down the draw, one of them even going into hiding almost a quarter mile from the others.

Now, coyotes were worth a dollar a head on the county market... that is the scalps were, the hides being worthless... and four dollars was quite a bit of money at that time of little work and poor wages. Gil needed the money. Being only a boy, I had no need for such a sum. Still, I was quite willing to lend Gil a hand in earning the amount then in sight.

"You stay here on the ridge and keep an eye on those babies to the right," said Gil. "Me an' old Buck will take that fellow on the left. When we get him, we'll come back for the rest of 'em."

The coyote on the left had scarcely settled himself for his morning nap when a dun thunderbolt tore across his bed. Desperately, he took off on a race for his life that ended an hour later at the end of a bridle rein...about half a mile from his bed. Full bellied, he had been an easy prey for the buckskin.

A little sprint of four or five miles, crowded all the way by the fresh

Chapter 6: About Some Horses and Their Riders

horse, and Gil dropped his saddle rope over the coyote's head. A few minutes later, the scalp... worth a silver dollar was dangling at old Buck's saddle bow.

The coyote, as is their nature, had run in a wide circle, ending up not far from the place of starting. From my place on the ridge, I was able to be in at the kill when at last they swung back on the home stretch.

"How's the others?" were Gil's first words as I rode up. "They still in bed?"

Assured that they were, he repaired to the ridge where I had been keeping watch. Loosing the saddle girths, he allowed old Buck a few bites of grass and a little time to get his breath.

"That fellow was pretty full of Henderson's chickens," he said. "Just couldn't seem to get goin'. Old Buck ran over him half a dozen times in the first mile! Them others are goin' to be a little harder to get to. But Buck's learnin' what we're after. They're sure goin' to have to stay out from under his feet...or git walked on!"

True to my uncle's predictions, Old Buck went after the next coyote with a vengeance. In the first mile the little buckskin ran over his prey twice...so bruising him up that his scalp was hanging at the saddle bow before the race was scarce begun.

By now, the day was warming up and the pony, while seemingly quite fresh, was beginning to lather under the saddle. While I stayed on the ridge, my uncle rode down in hopes of finding a pool of water. When he returned sometime later, we unsaddled and let the horses graze while we ate our own lunch.

"I imagine that's an old bitch an' a yearlin' pup," my uncle said, as we saddled up for the next run. "If I can get the bitch started first, you won't have so much trouble with the pup. It'll stay 'round here better'n the

Chapter 6: About Some Horses and Their Riders

old one. They're both in the dip together. You ride in there an' scatter 'em out. Maybe the bitch'll go first. I'd sure like to take a run at her while Old Buck is still fresh. She's apt to be some varmint to catch up with. Had all mornin' to rest and get rid of what she's done et. An' she's goin' to get plum away from that pup just as soon as she can."

He motioned toward the dip. "Give old Roney the leather now an' get 'em goin'. Pollow the pup, but don't crowd him any. Just watch where he goes, as' let him bed down again. I'll tend to him when I get back."

Well, I got old Roney into high gear and before they hardly knew what was up, we were down on them. As my uncle had surmised, the bitch broke cover first, heading off toward the west... bringing her quite near where my uncle and the buckskin waited. The pup didn't run very far, but slunk off up the dip a few hundred yards and went into hiding again.

Well past four o'clock a tired Gil and a much bedraggled buckskin pony came over the western hill whence they had disappeared several hours before. But there were three scalps hanging from the saddle bow.

"That bitch was sure hell for runnin," said my uncle. "Must have run her a good twenty miles. Run her clear south of Ness City. Never could turn her. She sure was stayin away from that pup. Just had to wear her plum out."

"Buck was so derned tired, he couldn't get on her when she finally did give up. She laid down behind a fence up there on Bert Ellis' west line. I couldn't get the fence down so's Buck could get over. So I finally had to kill her with a rock. Sure was some race!"

"But say, Kid, I done found the cattle we were lookin' for this mornin'. They're off up there by Petersillies. Been drinkin' at his tanks. You get on old Roney and hike up that way and get 'em started toward home. Soon's me and Buck have a little rest we're goin' to get that pup.

Chapter 6: About Some Horses and Their Riders

Then we'll come an' help you drive 'em in.

A little after sundown, we drove the cattle into the corral. When Gil pulled his saddle off the buckskin that night there were four scalps at the saddle bow!

7. Concerning Geese, Wild and Otherwise

'There's a goose for every gander," said old Granny Shaben.

Granny was one of those priceless souls, found in almost every community of the west... and without whom it seemed impossible for the community to function.

Three hundred and seventy-five boys and girls in those early years called her "Granny", and gave her a love next to their own mother. The number '375' she placed on my boy, John's, head when he of the third generation of Coles came to my house.

Three hundred and seventy-five babies delivered into the world, with never a casualty! And this by an unlettered old German woman who could scarcely write her name. This, in and under circumstances no modern doctor would even begin to consider. Is it any wonder that we of that time put a great deal of faith in what she told us! Or that we considered diligently the homey remarks and parables of this wise old woman!

Granny's 'goose an' gander' remark, made in a conversation with my mother... and concerning my Aunt Lizzie and Uncle George...still lingers in my memory when I think of the latter.

Uncle George de Void I am not even certain I ever saw. But, to this day, whenever I think of my aunt and uncle, I get a mental picture of a very high stepping young goose, followed about by a rancorous gander bent on pinching the legs of everyone who crossed their path.

This thought and feeling of mine may not have been entirely the fault of my uncle, but must, undoubtedly, have been helped along by my aunt's attitude in my later association with her. Uncle George himself, passed early from the picture. Two or three years, at the most, he stayed on the Golden Range... passing on then into the unknown countries of the

Chapter 7: Concerning Geese, Wild and Otherwise

west. My aunt never knew for sure what became of him.

When still a small boy I remember receiving a box of man's clothing from somewhere in Washington or Oregon with word of his death along with a request that she receive these as being his sole possessions before the law. My aunt always seemed to think that this was some kind of ruse to eat her out of property that might have been hers at his death. But having secured a divorce from him a few years before, she had to be satisfied with this and let the matter stand.

To this couple, I believe, was born the first grandchild of my grandparents on the Golden Range. A little girl named Pearly, who did not long survive in that land of sunshine... but went away early into another Land. It seems as though I can remember this little girl, but this might not be so. So easily are the memories of childhood confused the hearsay with the actual! But I am certain of visiting a small grave on the side of a hill and being told, "This is Pearly de Void's grave." And of wondering why the mound of earth when they had told me Pearly was in heaven.

Uncle George was a Frenchman, with all of a Frenchman' suaveness of manner, but with a great deal, too, of a gander s pertinacity. Especially concerning things amorous... and not in the least above an amoretto with others of the flock. Provided of course, this could be managed with no inconvenience to himself.

Grandpap Cole never let his feelings be known in the matter. But it is family history that he kept his weather eye open whenever the Frenchman was about. Especially if Aunt Lizzy was absent. The Cole girls were as fair as the average, and Grandpap had come a long way since the days of his youth. I have been told that Uncle George had at some time during his association with the Cole family, acquired a very wholesome respect for the hickory cane Pap Cole had carried all the way from Missouri.

Chapter 7: Concerning Geese, Wild and Otherwise

The corn crop of 1878 was gathered a few days before Christmas. Now the men of the Cole family, the price of their Fall wages in their pockets, turned homesick glances toward the stone dugout in the bank of the draw. Even as Grand Pap had predicted, the Golden Range had somehow become home to them... even though they had seen but a few days of its varying moods.

Having finished his work a few days before the others, Uncle George had hastened home on foot... rather than wait for the others and the wagon. He came in across the prairies from Alexander, having walked and ridden with other cornhuskers into that place... and from there coming on foot to the dugout.

My mother had never thought too much of Uncle George, having guessed his disposition... particularly where women were concerned. However, realizing that the others, including my father, could not be many days away, she received him with a warmth unusual in her dealings with him. At the moment the rest of the family were out on the prairie bringing in a load of fuel for the fires. Possibly wishing to misunderstand the motive of her handshake... and allowing more sentiment than the occasion demanded, he made advances that sent my mother fleeing the house.

Fortunately, she met the others who were just returning. Of course, she said nothing of the incident to either Grandma or Aunt Lizzy... thinking she might have been mistaken about the Frenchman's intentions.

A few days later the Frenchman came into the house unexpectedly when she was washing dishes. Catching her in his arms, he exclaimed, 'Now I have caught you, my little wild girl!"

Immediately she gave such an account of herself that Uncle George could not mistake her opinion of him and Frenchmen in general. With the wagon and returning corn huskers just then coming into sight across the flats to the east, Uncle George made haste to apologize. He had

Chapter 7: Concerning Geese, Wild and Otherwise

no desire to face my father, or Pap's hickory cane. For the family's sake, my Mother grudgingly forgave him. How the Frenchman managed to explain his badly scratched face and swollen eye to the family, I never heard.

Father never quite understood Mother's antipathy toward Uncle George, but Pap, being wiser, was not fooled. When a few days later my uncle and aunt were offered a home with a couple of bachelor brothers across the creek Pap insisted it might be best for all concerned if they accepted. Considering the crowded condition of the dugout plus the fact the brothers were offering room and board in exchange for Aunt Lizzie's services as a housekeeper. The matter being settled Pap said no more about it. But that night at supper Grand Ma was heard to mutter, "That George! I always knew Lizzie would drive her ducks to a poor market!"

It has always been a mystery to me why an unmarried man should be called an old 'batch', just because he lived alone and did his own housework... regardless of his age. Despite the fact that they were only twenty-four and twenty-six, respectively, Walter and George Mathis were 'old batches'. They lived alone and kept a house and were, therefore, so called and so considered by all the residents of the Golden Range country. But, somehow, their status changed when Uncle George and Aunt Lizzy went to live with them. Thereafter they were known simply as the Mathis boys. Such is the power of a woman in the house!

It was this same Walter Mathis who had met my people the summer before, somewhere in eastern Kansas, and directed them westward to the claims they later secured. He had known the relinquishments were for sale and had acted as agent for the two parties.

At Christmas time that year, now having a housekeeper and cook on the place, the Mathis boys insisted the Coles must spend the day with them. Interest was heightened by the fact that the boys had killed a couple

Chapter 7: Concerning Geese, Wild and Otherwise

of wild geese, caught pilfering a field of rice corn on the creek bottoms. Aunt Lizzy was to do the honors and the entire family were expected to be there...Santa Claus and all.

On the afternoon of the twenty-fourth the first storm of the year blew in from the north and Pap Cole thought it best to keep his Christmas at home in the dugout. Only my father, mother, and Aunt Jenny braved the storm to the Mathis' house. Becoming lost, they wandered about over the prairie until at last, deep in the darkness of the night, they stumbled upon the Mathis house in the bank of the creek.

If you would have the story complete, read "My First Christmas in Kansas," by my mother, Mrs. John Cole, Ness County News.

8. Some Landmarks

Winter is bitter and merciless on the prairies. But if it be withheld until after the first of the year, there comes with every storm the promise of the spring. Before that time, there is the hopelessness of autumn and the early storm holds no promise. Half dried leaves on tree and bush. Buffalo grass still green at the base... with the corn of its summer crop still in the milk. Straggling wild fowl lingering around the scattered water holes, caught in the grip of some early storm... These things speak always of death and disaster.

Not so the storm that is delayed until after the wild bird has gone away and the dried leaf has settled down into a spongy bead at root of tree and bush, and the crisp, yellow grass has become bent with age that ripens and prepares its corn for the gendering of another crop.

There is hope in this. And the very winds that drive relentlessly across the miles speak a new life and sing a new song. The larder may be empty, the fodder pile a ghost of its former self, the cow chins for the fire buried deep in snow and the wind may howl with a vehemence undreamed of in the autumn, but, somehow, there was hope on the prairies. And the dweller there took courage from this hope and said to himself: It will soon be spring.

In that year of 1878, the first storm of winter came late in the season. Although it found the family in the stone dugout almost penniless, it brought the first faint hint of spring, with its hopes and promises. Scarcely had the snow ceased falling when the men and boys were down along the creek, cutting wood and ricking it against the day when it could be hauled to Dodge or Hayes and traded for provisions. As the storm had spoken of the springtime, the older men began to think of seeds for field and garden... and implements to till the prairie soil. And they, too, taking

Chapter 8: Some Landmarks

courage of hope, said:

"It will soon be spring."

Just how much the Coles owe to the Mathis family will probably never be paid; or even computed. For instance, the Mathis boys... having a contract for wood to be delivered to either one of the forts at Dodge or Hays... generously allowed the Cole men to cut and haul as much of that wood as they might. They even furnished the wood from their own abundant supply along the creek, asking but a trifle for the same.

Eight dollars per cord, delivered to Dodge fifty miles away... Uncle Sam did everything in his power to win his bet with the homesteader! However, my people were thankful for the market and have always thought a great deal of the at his family for the opportunity thus offered them. With all the men working, a load was ready for the trip to Dodge every two or three days. Two days there, two days back... and eight dollars worth of provisions for a family of fourteen! Fortunately, they didn't have to pay income tax. And the horses could forage on the buffalo grass, forced to be content with its scanty crop of corn for grain.

"We knew we could make it if none of us got sick," I have heard my father say. "And if the horses were always able to make the trip, for the market was there. But, sometimes, in order to reach it we had to take two or three wagons at a time. That way we could double up in crossing the creeks and draws."

On one of these trips to Hays in 1879 my father had the misfortune to catch his scanty clothing on fire while getting breakfast over a camp fire. Thereafter... with the seat and front of his jeans being gone...he must needs be very polite, always holding his big range hat in front while addressing anyone, and behind while retiring! This he was forced to do until he returned home where Grandmother could patch them.

Chapter 8: Some Landmarks

Another time that spring while taking a load of lime burned in a kiln in the back of the creek to Hays, he got caught in a heavy spring rain. Having nothing with which to cover his lime, the same went into slack, setting fire to the wagon and completely destroying the lime. With no provisions at home, he proceeded to the Fort where he spent his last sixty cents for a sack of corn meal. But spring was coming on and there was song in the air, so he hurried back for another load of wood or lime.

Old time freighters have told me of seeing the pile of slacked lime and rocks on the banks of the Smoky Hill River near Fort Hays. I suppose it might still be there if one could find the oil trail into the place... a mute reminder of pioneer endeavor. The freighters called this pile of rock, "John's Folly," and used it as a landmark on the road to Hays. Father called it, "John's Disappointment."

Then there was the story of freighter Stokes who that first springtime was freighting into Hays with my father and several others. Hauling wood, they chose to travel in company that they might double teams on the hard pulls. One of the four had a tarpaulin cover over his wagon, a handy arrangement when the rains came. The others of the company used this covered wagon for sleeping quarters, thus avoiding beds on the wet ground.

Friend Stokes always a little weak toward hard liquor, had managed to take on quite a jag in the afternoon before starting home. That night, camped along the Smoky in a cold, chilling rain, Stokes felt the need to relieve himself.

Seeking to ease himself, Stokes lifted the flap of the wagon cover... letting in a flood of wind and rain on the other sleepers.

After a reasonable time, one of the men admonished Stokes to hurry up and close the flap. Being still somewhat under influence of John Barleycorn, the freighter could not understand the trickling sound of the

Chapter 8: Some Landmarks

rain down the wagon track.

Therefore, he remained for some time in the same position, and still holding the flap of the wagon cover open.

By now, the entire group was demanding he shut the flap and get back into bed. This only increased his confusion.

Finally he called plaintively to my father: "John, won't you please come here and give me a hand. I can't get the derned thing to quit!"

The freighters afterward called that particular camp, "Stokes' Confusion."

Another time this same Stokes, while taking a load of hay into Dodge had the drunken misfortune to upset the load on a hill. In the process, he managed to get himself caught under the rack.

Accompanying him at the time was a son, who had been trained to obey him without question. Therefore when Stokes, being in considerable pain and thinking his time had come, ordered the boy to set fire to the hay and put him out of his misery, the obedient lad did just that!

Had not another freighter happened along just then, the drunken Stokes would have entered the hereafter by a very fiery route. As it was, a considerable prairie fire was started... and a good freight wagon destroyed. This spot on the road was hereafter known as, "Stoke's Despair.'

Thus, the great in those days left reminders of their efforts and presence on the prairies... much as the great have done through all time and in all places.

9. About the Springtime

Benard De Voto has called 1846 the year of decision, intimating that in that year, more people moved out of the east across the Mississippi and onto the Great Plains than in any other year, before or after. However that might be, I know that it was all of thirty years later before that great tidal wave of humanity spread over the Golden Range country of western Kansas. And, as a spent wave... pushed forward by the oncoming tide... settling into the black soil of that far-flung shore.

<u>1846 - 1876.</u>

Thirty years of sunshine and solitude. Thirty years of dreamy, hopeless autumn times. Thirty years of biting, blinding winters. And never a soul to break the prairie soil or scatter a handful of seed for harvest.

A hunter now and then, chasing the last of the buffalo into the sun. An immigrant wagon, winding its lonely way into Oregon or dipping down into the golden Californias. A feverish Morman, racing across the miles to lose himself among his brethern on the bleak shores of the Great Salt Lake.

But never a settler for the best land of them all; the Golden Range.

Thirty years of uncertainty and doubt and deep mystery.

Thirty years of wave on wave sweeping over the most fertile land in all the world. And then, at last, in 1876, the spent seventh... as it were... falling short on the most gracious portion of that vast shore line.

A dugout in the bank of a draw was not much to attract the eye when one looked across a fifty mile stretch of undulating prairie. A tumble weed, moving in the morning breeze, might attract a great deal more attention. But it, too, would soon be lost in the distance.

Chapter 9: About the Springtime

A tree... A tree was quite another matter. In 1876-1878, a tree spoke of something fixed, something permanent, something to tie to. And beyond that it meant even more. It meant water in a land where water was scarce and hard to find. It meant a place where a man might dig and find and quench his thirst. Sometimes, it meant a spring, where wild things came at night that they might drink and live another day. A place where the hot sun of summer might be defied. And wild things came, even at noontide, to rest and cool themselves.

Hunters went often to the trees of the prairies, for wild life seemed to congregate there, and hunting was thus more profitable. Also, trees meant wood, as well as water, and game and rest and cool. On the prairies, they were priceless. And it was where -trees grew that the first wave of immigration fixed itself, and where it stayed longest.

Pap Cole had guided himself and caravan by memory to that lone tree on the ridge, where once a spring of pure water had flowed. And then there was the creek nearby where wood and water could be had in plenty.

A cottonwood, near a waterhole on Jenny's homestead, grew into a considerable grove that still flourishes and is the pride of the whole countryside.

Between the divide, where this tree grew, and the dugout in the bank of the draw, was another tree. There the Coles found one of their first neighbors, a Mr. Kirk. However, they did not know it that first autumn...a dugout being hard to distinguish on the prairies.

It was along the creek that they found the most settlement the first winter. And it was there the settlement longest continued. For wood and water were there and a measure of shelter from the winter winds. Today, men have driven drills through the black soil of the uplands, deep into the underflow, and have found springs of living water. But in those days, it had to be found along the creek or along the draws that came in from the

Chapter 9: About the Springtime

divide.

As Grand Pap Cole had said, it wasn't long before there was a settler on every quarter section of that vast country. The coming of spring brought another wave of settlement. Neighbors became so plentiful as almost to become a nuisance.

Up the draw on the next quarter adjoining my father's, a fellow by the name of O'Neil built a little one room stone house that stood there on the valley floor for full fifty years... although the O'Neils themselves did not tarry long. O'Neil, some sort of teacher with a considerable account in an eastern bank, came only to secure a piece of Kansas land. As soon as the claim was proved up, he went back to his teaching.

When her first sod house was built, my mother went one day to visit this O'Neil woman. When she returned from her visit, she was very much enriched by the gift of an empty tomato can and a square of pine board to cut meat on.

"I sure felt I was getting along in the world," Mother said in telling me of the incident. "A twelve by fourteen sod house, all my own, a hundred and sixty acres of Kansas land... and this fine beginning of household goods!"

Spring came first along the creek that year, as it usually does on the Golden Range. The boys, Cass and Jake, found the first green things growing along the northern banks, where the ice was beginning to give place to the returning sun.

Little blue violets and wild white mustard and the first tender shoots of the artichoke and the green chokeberry.

Grand Ma Cole sent them back with a basket to gather the mustard for greens. And an old Indian scout told them how to dig under the dead leaves for the artichoke, a dainty morsel in the springtime.

Chapter 9: About the Springtime

Young cottontail rabbits there were, too... born in February. By the first of April they were ready for the frying pan. Also, the boys caught some coon... and a possum. In Virginia such game was considered 'ni***r food', but here it rated considerably higher and was accepted with thankful hearts.

Along the draw, they found some yellow Johnnie-jump-ups. And among the stalks of last year's sunflowers, a great promise for the gold of another summer... young sunflowers.

The rocky slope back of the dugout and the flats where they picked the pretty rocks were soon warmed by the springtime sun...and spread themselves to beat the creek with the returning color.

Yellow daisies strong and rancid in odor, but beautiful in petal and shade. Wind flowers, hiding behind the rocks. Dainty, white cat tails and wild, yellow flax.

Yellow seemed the prevailing color along the slopes and the hills were soon ready to declare Pap's title of 'Golden Range'.

The Cole girls, along with my mother, the stranger among them, were wild with delight at the beauty that spread itself over the prairie, along the creek and over the hillsides and rocky flats that first spring. Now the melancholy of the autumn seemed as a bad dream of the long ago.

The old scout taught them how to find the bread roots the Indian women used for food; and how to tell the difference between the buffalo peas and the rattle weeds that were so much alike. The peas were splendid food, but the rattle weeds were poisonous. The Loco weed was of this family and later in the season caused a great deal of trouble among the livestock. He also showed them how to tell a mushroom from a toad-stool, and taught them where and when these dainty fungi might be found.

Remembering Missouri and the wild strawberries of the woods,

Chapter 9: About the Springtime

my Mother looked long and carefully along the creek and among the tassels of the blooming buffalo grass for the berries, but found not a single one. She did find a great number of round, ball-like cactus, full to overflowing with bright red berries, hidden in the grass. The old scout taught her how to gather the fruit with a knitting needle or a sharpened stick. Eating them, her lips grew red and her breath sweet and pungent... and it was not hard to make believe she was eating the homeland berries.

The jackrabbit plow, a little thing of rod and lay, was gotten ready and soon a long, black furrow reached its length' across the lower forty. Potatoes, corn for roasting ears, and cane for sorghum were planted. Grand Ma and the girls had a garden just beyond the little mound back of the house.

The old man planted tobacco, brought from Missouri, and tried a few cotton seeds. But melons, squash, big field pumpkins and cimlins were the better crop and made a great showing all through the spring and summer and late into the fall.

The big wallow on the upper forty filled with melting snow and became a madhouse of squawking geese, quacking duck and rendezvous for every manner of wading and swimming bird known to the west. Old Betsy was kept warm those days with many a fine dinner supplied from that source.

Yes, it was springtime on the Golden Range and the Coles were quite content.

10. About Some Neighbors

As Pap Cole had predicted it was not long until there was a family on almost every quarter section of the Golden Range. Not that they stayed very long or made themselves very conspicuous. But they came and their numbers were legion, and they went on and were forgotten.

A mound of earth where the soddy stood, sometimes three or four to the quarter section. Or a hole in the bank of the draw, or on the level land where the dugout had been. In a few years time this was all that remained of their passing.

Their very names were forgotten. Or remembered only by a few of those too poor to get away. Or who, like Pap Cole, had reached the land of their dreams.

Of those who stayed, the third and fourth generations still sound the names of those old times. And a look at the county records seems to say, Old Timer or Pioneer when these names are encountered. Many of those who came in '78, '79, or '80, however, went away early, leaving no mark on the prairies nor name on the record book. It took five years to prove to Uncle Sam that one meant business. And five years was a long time at playing make-believe. At pretending the homestead was a bit of Missouri or Iowa or Vermont or York state... or some other place.

"Young blood," Grand Pap said, "must make the Golden Range. For the Golden Range is a new land and sufficient unto itself." He had learned that first year that this was not Virginia, even as others learned it was not York state, nor Vermont, nor even Missouri. Thereafter he planted no more tobacco, but increased his fields of sorghum and rice corn and even tried a little spring and winter wheat.

Still the neighbors came and went. We learned the names of a great many of them, and as quickly forgot them as they passed on. The few that

Chapter 10: About Some Neighbors

stayed became as one family and their doings were long remembered and often recounted among us. The years have made us one clan, if not one family, for those who stayed had to find husbands and wives on the Golden Range... and not in York state nor Virginia. Those places were far removed in the 80s and '90s.

The Coles lived in the first big draw west of Alexander and thought they had the choice quarter section of all that big country. The Castles lived around the brow of the hill to the north and west. They had dugout near the old cottonwood that had served Pap Cole as a landmark when he returned to the Range after thirty years. Some distance further on was the home of one Dennis Hurley, an almost blind Irishman. An old batch, without family or connection, Dennis, like thousands of others, had drifted to this new land in search of a home.

I have often wondered how the physically handicapped, such as Dennis Hurley, found the courage to combat their infirmities, along with the natural obstacles placed in their path. That they did and left a reminder of their sojourn on the prairies, is a recorded fact. Not only was this reminder left in the hearts and memories of their neighbors, but in the homes they built and the lands they tamed. In the enduring monument of wells dug or groves started... or some other permanent writing on the open scroll of the prairies.

Having no livestock Dennis... a neighbor of both the Coles and the Castles... turned to the soil and his two hands for a living. A considerable garden spot had been dug up around his one room sod house. As the season advanced, the garden became green with vegetables.

Now Castle had a very ambitious cow who insisted on paying this garden an occasional visit. Especially when the gardener was absent or too far removed to see clearly. Several times she had damaged both the garden and the usually sunny disposition of the good natured Irishman. Dennis

Chapter 10: About Some Neighbors

had protested to both the cow and his neighbor, Castle, with indifferent results.

At last his patience exhausted, he bethought himself of the old army musket behind the soddy. door. Not having shot with which to load... and being exceedingly short on powder... he put a small amount of the latter in the old gun, and rammed home a long strip of bacon rind in lieu of shot.

The cow, having had no experience with such things, and holding half blind men in contempt, ignored Dennis. Grimly, he squeezed the trigger. The old musket burst forth with a bellow of smoke and sound. An even louder bellow burst from the cow as a flaming piece of salty bacon rind seared her hide from the root of her stubborn tail to the base of her crumpled horn! Departing immediately, she never stopped until well in the shelter of the Castle dooryard.

The supposition is that the cow was more scared than hurt. However, the salty rind had left a bloody scar her entire length. A scar that must have been a bit painful as well as appearing of a serious nature.

Hearing the shot... and seeing the dramatic result of it... Castle, in high dudgeon, stomped across the half mile of prairie to the Hurley cabin.

"You bloody Irishman!" he shouted. "What do you mean by shooting my cow? And just how in hell did you do so much damage to her?"

Standing in the soddy door, squinting through half blind eyes, the Irishman began reloading his ancient musket.

"Neighbor Castle, you know blame well why I shot that derned old cow of yours," he said calmly. "As for how scorched her hide...why, I shot her with a piece of bacon rind.

"Now, I got only one more load of powder an' this little piece of

Chapter 10: About Some Neighbors

bacon rind left." His face never changed expression. "I'm loadin' up with it, Castle. An' if you ain't off 'n the place time I get through, I'm goin' to let you have it, same as the cow."

Castle wasn't in sight when the rind was pushed home.

On the far divide... beyond and a bit to the west of the Cole dugout... was a considerable settlement of German and Swiss people. All spoke Low German among themselves, but English or American with the rest of the countryside. We of the creekbottoms and this side of the divide, were wont to call this settlement 'Little Germany', and the people there of, Dutchmen.

To the west of this people and beyond the divide was a considerable settlement of Catholic Irish, known as South Ireland. North Ireland was another like community, but on the north of the creek... and well away toward the divide in that direction. These were wonderful people, indispensible to the settlement of the Golden Range. Their children and grandchildren still carry on the old family names and traditions. However, they have long been forgotten as 'Irish' or 'Dutch'. Now, as Pap Cole had wished, they are just plain American folk, with no Mason or Dixon line, nor any other line separating them.

Early that summer, Emil Mauth, a young German from this settlement, asked my father for the loan of a team of ponies and a light rig. It seemed he was to meet and bring home as bride a young woman just arrived in Hays from the old country.

"I have no money to pay for the use of the team, Herr Cole," he said, "But you may use my yoke of cattle instead of the ponies while I am gone.'

This suited my father very well. He had some heavy hauling to be done, and the oxen would serve the purpose much better than the light

Chapter 10: About Some Neighbors

team of horses. And, certainly, the horses would serve young Mauth much better on the road.

With Emil Mauth well on his way to Hays and happiness, my father hitched the oxen, a young and high lived pair, to the wagon's running gears and started toward the creek. He had a load of logs in mind to haul. He didn't get very far in that direction.

Emil had broken the oxen to the German language; they understood nothing else. Hence, Mauth had instructed father in the proper commands in that language. But not being very good at languages, Father somehow got his terms confused... with disastrous results.

When he ordered the oxen to stop, they only went the faster! Thinking to correct the situation by shouting louder, he soon had the oxen going at a good fast trot. A little later, being young and full of go, they broke into a run! Without lines to guide the beasts and having forgotten every word Mauth had taught him, Father soon found himself and the team approaching their home corral atop the divide. Many miles from the log pile on the creek!

Completely at a loss as to Low German, my father unyoked the oxen, all the time blistering them with a wide range of good, pungent English. -Then, turning them loose in the home pasture, he walked the four or five miles to the dugout... content to do without a team until Mauth's return. In after years he laughingly said he did it all for the good of the country... the Mauths begetting several children who, at this time, are of the nobility of the land.

Then there is the story that old man Mooney used to tell of the young Irishman, Tommy O'Brien, from over South Ireland way. It seems that Mr. Mooney was riding along on that side of the divide one summer day when he saw a funeral procession approaching. Not having heard of any recent deaths he was naturally curious as to which of his neighbors

Chapter 10: About Some Neighbors

had passed on.

In those days, the corpse was usually, carried in the coffin to the graveyard on a light wagon, the driver of the wagon sitting on the end of the rough box. Now it so happened that Mr. Mooney, approaching the procession, perceived his young friend, Tommy O'Brien, driving the 'hearse'. Not wishing to create a disturbance, Mooney rode alongside and quietly asked the Irishman whom the dead might be.

"Why, sure an' it's the man in the box!" retorted Tommy, touching the horses with the toe of his boot and driving on.

Albeit they were the very best of neighbors, the North Ireland folks were known as the 'Fightin' Irish'... title to which they somehow managed to live up to quite well.

They tell the story on the McGaughey brothers, living in that neighborhood, who had not seen one another for thirty years. Charley came to the Golden Range country early, in its history. Settling on a homestead a few miles west of McCracken, he eventually became a wheat farmer of considerable reputation.

Years later, grey haired and faltering of step, he received word his brother, Jim was coming from the Old Country to pay him a visit. Delighted beyond measure, Marley and his wife, Mary, rid up the old farm and laid in a supply of provisions.

On a Saturday, Charley met the train at McCracken and proudly bore his brother, Jim, back to the farm and the waiting Mary. After the handshakes and the first reminiscences were over, Mary repaired to the kitchen to prepare supper. Charley proposed that he and Jim have a look at the farm he had spent so many years acquiring.

Some time later, they sat down in the shade of a big cottonwood to rest.

Chapter 10: About Some Neighbors

"Sure, an' its bin a long day since you and me sat on a log togither, Jim," said Charley. "How well I remimber the day. It was just before I left for Ameriky."

"Sure,' said Jim. "An' you always was the stubborn cuss. Remimber how I had to lick th' hell out o' you that day whin you would be takin' me picture o' Mary O'Tool along wid ye?"

"It's a damn lie!" swore Charley. "Ye niver saw the day ye cud lick the likes o' me, Jim McGaughey!"

"Ha!" jeered his brother. "I did it the moiny a time, an' can do it agin when iver I plaze!"

"Be gittin' yerself ready thin," said Charley. "Let's see what ye kin do!"

Mary had to part the two of them when she came to call them to supper.

11. The Baileys

My Uncle Bill Bailey came into this world almost three hundred years too late. He should have been allowed to live out his life amidst the splendor of 'castle wall and snowy summit old in story'. A grand character, he, for one of Scott's novels or some grand old poem such as <u>The Lay of the Last Minstrel</u> or <u>The Lady of the Lake</u>. Certainly, to me, he seemed always to embody some character of those olden times. And, as a boy, after any contact with Uncle Bill, I always felt like writing romantic poetry for several days thereafter.

Probably he did not affect others of the family in like manner. As I recall, there was always considerable controversy among the Cole clan as to just where to place "W.T."... as-most of the men folk called him.

If the others of us were confused about this, not so Uncle Bill. He seemed not in the least worried about the day or place in which he might find himself. He went about the matter of living with never a thought of the morrow, supremely satisfied to let things take care of themselves. Sufficient unto the day, seemed his motto, and I never knew him to deviate in any manner from that motto.

A little man, he somehow gave the impression of being much larger than he really was. This was, I think, due to his habit of wearing his slightly greying hair (I never knew Uncle Bill when his hair was not slightly greying) in long curls reaching almost to his shoulders. His beard was also allowed a certain amount of liberty, covering his boyish face in a manner suggesting its wearer's supreme indifference to beards in general... and this one in particular. Yet I have known Uncle Bill to sit by the fire in the soddy and allow us children the happy privilege of combing out and arranging this truculent beard to our fancy. And never once did he complain, no matter how long the operation might take.

Chapter 11: The Baileys

Truculent seems hardly the word to use in speaking of Uncle Bill, or of anything pertaining to him. For, like Moses of old, he was one of the meekest men of his day. And if his beard seemed fierce at times, it was due, in great measure, to the prairie winds and his supreme indifference to such things. Certain of my cousins contended this curly beard lent a dignity to Uncle Bill that a stronger beard had not accomplished. They may have been entirely right, for there never lived a more gentle, kindlier man than he.

Between Pap Cole and Uncle Bill there was a certain affinity not noticeable where the other sons-in-law were concerned. However, one had to be well acquainted with both to be aware of this, for Pap was certainly no respecter of persons.

"Bailey", as he generally called my uncle (the others said W.T.), was the one Confederate of the lot. This may have accounted for the mutual feeling of understanding between the two. How long Uncle Bill may have served the lost cause, I am not certain, nor in what capacity... for he must have been a mere boy in those days. However, I have heard him tell of incidents in which he took part that have since then become history.

Possibly he put in a few months with Pike or some other of the western leaders. That he was well acquainted with the guerrilla, Quantrell, I am sure... for I have heard him tell of riding a mission for his superior to Quantrell's camp.

Again, he spoke of taking provisions to the James and Younger boys when they were hiding somewhere in the hills of western Missouri. Some one of the women folk of his family, I believe, was married to one of the outlaws. Uncle Bill never said much about those days, content to let the past take care of itself while he went about the living of today.

Born in Virginia before the war, Aunt Molly was the oldest of the

Chapter 11: The Baileys

Cole children. She was married to 'Mr. Bailey', as she always called him, when the family moved from Virginia to western Missouri. My aunt was a very gentle natured woman kind and good to all about her, and we of the second generation of prairie Coles loved her dearly. However, she had a habit of looking after her own that was sometimes very exasperating to us children. Especially on Christmas, or any of the other feast days observed by the clan.

Most of us had been taught to fend for ourselves when it came to anything to eat. But to ask for something between meals was not to be considered. Not so, the Bailey youngsters. No matter when or where they asked Aunt Molly always secured a bite for them. This, of course, led to a certain amount of hard feeling among us, since we were always hungry. To be discriminated against in this manner... and about so vital a matter... we just couldn't understand it. Therefore, we went about correcting the offense in a manner of our own that sometimes left bloody noses and ruffled plumage.

Aunt Molly was the money-maker of the family. Uncle Bill, not being much concerned about such matters preferred to let the lady of the house take care of such mercenary things as finance. Too, he always contended Molly had the education for such things, having- been a school teacher when he found and married her. To my knowledge, Uncle Bill never looked at book or paper, not that there were very many of such things on the prairies. But he did have a wonderful repertoire of songs and stories to his credit. These made him excellent company in any crowd.

Not so, Aunt Molly. My strongest memory of her is her sitting in some corner, a book or magazine in her hand... regardless of date or kind of publication. Sitting and reading while her hostess prepared the meal.

Although very kind and gentle in her ways, she was of a very nervous nature. In her case, I have always considered her nervousness a

Chapter 11: The Baileys

disease. She had a considerable goiter on her throat that bothered her all her later life. Always we boys were kept on the watch for a green snake...something unknown on the prairies...that she might wrap around her neck to frighten the goiter away. Had we been able to produce the snake, I have no doubt Aunt Molly would have tried the remedy, just to please us.

We had the story among us of how, when but a girl of eleven, Aunt Molly had been pitted against some of the best rifle shots in Virginia in a shooting match.

It seems a number of men and boys were shooting at a target when Pap and his daughter, Molly, happened by. The shooting had been pretty good, as it usually was among those people, but Pap laughingly chided the best shot among them for having barely entered the bullseye...instead of centering it.

"If I couldn't do better'n that, I'd quit," he said.

Quietly, the contestant handed him the gun. "You do better an' you can have the prize. Four or five dollars."

Pap only laughed at him. "Why, this little girl of mine can beat that shot of yours in the target!"

Handing the gun to Molly, he told her to show the crowd what real shootin' was like.

After loading the gun and taking sight at the target, Aunt Molly calmly set the gun down.

"I'm too nervous," she said. "Just wait a minute."

Moments later, she lifted the heavy squirrel rifle to her shoulder and drove dead center to the target!

The Baileys did not get to the Golden Range the same time as the

Chapter 11: The Baileys

other Coles. Somewhere in eastern Kansas, they stopped off to visit friends. Finding work, they tarried there until early the following summer. Once they arrived, however, it did not take them long to find a spot to their liking. Actually Pap had already found a place for them, just a mile or so up the draw. This was still much below where Jenny had chosen to build her 'castle', although it was a year or two later before her dream came true.

Had they built a house above ground, it might have been seen from the Cole dugout. But Uncle Bill, never very ambitious, was quite content to follow the usual manner of building in those days, and went underground. Aunt Molly, who had visions of a stone house above ground, was never quite content until she realized her wish several years later.

The first Bailey dugout, as I remember it was a pretentious affair, having two rooms with a stone partition between. A bit of inconvenience in bad weather, true. However, we children rather liked it that way. For when put to bed in one room, we romped about as much as we liked without disturbing the older folks in the other part of the house.

The roof was of log and willow, a much better arrangement than most of the early day houses. The willows were a product of the Bailey homestead, a great clump of the marsh variety growing along the draw in front of the dugout.

Another advantage of the Bailey place was the presence of sand, a very scarce commodity... even in that big country. Thus, my uncle became one of the country's first bankers. A sand banker.

This sand bank of Uncle Bill's was peculiar, in that it was a carry over from another age; and a very ancient age at that. Just why it should be in that particular spot, I have often wondered. I have even asked several geologists, but have yet to be satisfied with any of their answers. Unlike other sand, this was composed of ancient shells and fish and shark's teeth... and little globular bits of rocks resembling mother of pearl. And,

Chapter 11: The Baileys

sometimes, what looked like pearls themselves.

We children liked nothing better than to spend a day in this old pit. Especially if there were men taking out the sand. Then we always came away with an astonishing collection of ancient things.

Uncle Bill received as much as fifty cents per yard for this sand in the pit. Judging from the size of the pit as the years went by, he must have realized a considerable sum from sale of ancient things. A little side draw, coming in from the prairies toward the west, had this accumulation of sand for one bank. Years later, when the sand was at last all hauled away, we boys made a grand swimming hole in the pit by damming up the draw below and catching the summer rains.

The Baileys brought three children with them from Missouri; Alice, Arthur and Susie. John and Buela were products of the Golden Range. A little girl named Clara came, too, but did not tarry long. She was buried beside the other little mound on the hillside. In those days, this quiet spot was known as the Frank Hand graveyard, but has long since been discontinued, as, indeed, have many others on those sunny slopes. I doubt now if one might find it at all, so soon do those things pass away... even in the memory of Man... if they are not attended to.

One thing Uncle Bill brought with him from Missouri that always interested we boys of the later generation was an old double barreled shot gun. A muzzle loader. If there was powder and shot and caps for the gun we could always get Uncle Bill to go hunting. Many a fine days sport we have had... driving about over the prairie in the old spring wagon.

Game was abundant. Wild duck, prairie chicken and rabbits galore. Coyote and kit fox, and, in earlier years, a few antelope. But we were never able to get close enough to these latter to make a kill. We had to be content to watch them disappear from the prairies as had the buffalo before them. In addition, there were countless smaller game of the west on the prairies;

Chapter 11: The Baileys

and we generally brought home a load when we went out. I can still see my uncle, a bunch of us youngsters in the wagon beside him; standing up, with one of us for driver and others for retrievers, driving through the lagoons and wallows shooting ducks, curlews or snipes, as the case might be. And, sometimes, a goose or brant thrown in for good measure.

Particularly do I remember the day when he shot a Golden Eagle. Breaking its wing, Uncle Bill thought to capture it alive. But in trying to place a cord around the eagle's leg, he somehow allowed the creature to sink its talons in his hand. It was necessary to kill the bird before we could pry the talons out of Uncle Bill's hand. A painful, as well as difficult job... the eagle having driven his talons completely through and clenched them on the other side.

This Uncle Bill of mine could always be depended upon for a hunt, or to go fishing, or to take a day off for a picnic... or most any of the things that were of interest to boys. It is not to be wondered that we loved him with a love but little short of worship.

However, I would not leave the impression that the Baileys were a careless set. For this would be far from the truth. Uncle Bill always managed to have plenty to eat in the house. Even if he did get a great deal of it from the prairies in the way of game and fish and the wild things that lived there. His corn was always the best, if not the largest, in the country. And we prairie kids knew that there would be a melon patch hidden away somewhere in the shady depths... and that just so long as we were reasonably careful of the vines, we were welcome to the fruit.

Aunt Molly was the money maker of the family and could drive home as close a bargain as any of the traders of the times. While Uncle Bill sang his songs and grew his corn and melons and went hunting with us youngsters, she was adding continually to the herd of fine cattle and horses that was wealth on the Golden Range.

Chapter 11: The Baileys

And then, her house came at last... built above ground, as she had dreamed, near a beautiful box elder grove my uncle planted the first year he was on the claim. This house was paid for in cash from Aunt Molly's stocking, we kids were led to believe... there being no banks she would trust at the time!

Ah, but the Baileys were wonderful people!

12. Ante Bellum Days

Pap Cole had six boys, of whom my father was the oldest. Willie died when but a baby in Virginia; the others grew to manhood on the Golden Range. Being the oldest my father could well remember when six Negroes called him 'Master'. That was in the days before the war, before Pap lost everything, along with the Negroes.

One old colored fellow by the name of Jake, plus his two wives and their children, was the special property of my father. Jake, being the freighter for the plantation and a master at such things, taught Father how to handle a four or six horse team. He would also take him, as a very small boy alongside him on the seat of the big freight wagon loaded with plantation produce, and be gone from home several days at a time. Always careful of the boy's welfare, Jake taught him all he knew about horses and mules, as well as freighting. Possibly, it was this early training that made my father such a good horseman and trader in later years.

Old Jake saw to it that 'Marse John' learned all that he knew of a great variety of things, even teaching him a few bars on the fiddle... and a great number of plantation songs. Story has it that old Jake used to get one wife upstairs in the cabin and the other downstairs while he sat midway on the steps between... fiddling to keep the two from a family brawl!

On the many trips to market, Jake, as overseer, commanded the Negro boys who drove or went along to help load and/or unload. Although Father was too young to know much about the business end of things, he could remember any number of queer escapades these Negro boys were continually getting themselves into. And, in later years, he often delighted us boys with tales of old Jake's adventures.

One of the most hilarious of these yarns centered around a fine new pop-gun a young colored boy bought for my father. Now old Jake

Chapter 12: Ante Bellum Days

cautioned 'Marse John' on how, when and where to use the gun... and made certain that he did no mischief with it. But the young fellows who drove the other wagons had a great deal of fun with the gun. Occasionally they borrowed it to scare one of the numerous Negroes about the wagon yard or in the towns where they stopped.

Unfortunately, Jake did not have eyes in the back of his head. Therefore it was inevitable that, sooner or later, my father should 'let go' at somebody with his weapon. When he finally did, he chose a lovely target... and he didn't miss. The results were...most exciting.

It happened on the outskirts of Charlottsville. 'Marse John' was in the feed box on the back end of old Jake's wagon, a favorite perch of his. Hence, from the driver's seat, Jake could not see what the boy was doing. Pleasantly relaxed, he had no premonition of trouble as the heavily loaded wagon rumbled past a pretentious house where a young peoples' party was in progress.

At that moment, an elegantly dressed young lady sitting just inside the window, caught sight of the passing caravan. The picture of old Jake on the driver's seat, apparently unaware of the little white boy stealing a ride in the back evidently struck her as supremely funny. Laughing, she stuck her head out the window for a better look, then popped it back inside to joke with her friends. Another moment, and Jake's wagon would have left the house behind. But the Devil, in the form of the Negro boy on the following wagon, flashed 'Marse John' a white-toothed smile. Then whipping an imaginary gun to his shoulder, he aimed it at the now-empty window, sang out 'Pow!' and then nodded his head vigorously.

Marse John caught on fast. But feeling the distance too great for accurate shooting, he slipped off the box and, running up underneath the window, waited for the girl's head to reappear. When it did, he pulled the trigger. A bright red spot popped out on the soft, white chin thrust out so

Chapter 12: Ante Bellum Days

tantalizingly just above his head. The cork must have really stung! With a startled scream, the girl ducked back inside, banging her head against the window in her haste.

Marse John tore back to the wagon and jumped into the feed box. Old Jake, lost in his own thoughts, never even turned. He had missed the entire 'drama'. In the following wagon, the black-skinned Devil bent over, convulsed with laughter. Afterward, he told my father how a great passel of white folks came boiling out of the house, searching every crack and cranny for the marksman. No one had even so much as suspected the cute little white boy in the feed box of the wagon!

In Charlottsville, where the Cole plantation sold most of its produce, a group of city Negroes had a habit of jumping the country boys when they came to town. Although Jake tried to avoid these hoodlums, he was not always successful. Frequently, he either had to fight or take a lickin'. Finally becoming tired of this, he begged my grandfather to let him take several of the plantation's younger men into town... 'jes' fo' one trip'. Being a Deacon in the local Baptist church, Jake did not want Pap to know the reason behind his request. Therefore, he simply implied that he wanted the young men to see for themselves the 'wickedness' of the city. That way, he explained, they would be a lot more content with plantation life. Since there was a lull in the farm work just then, Pap somewhat reluctantly consented.

"But mind you," he warned Jake, "Keep them boys in hand an' out of trouble! An' no likker! You understand?"

Jake understood.

When the wagons pulled out the next time for Charlottsville, most of the young bucks of the Cole Plantation went along. Arriving in town, Jake kept his boys out of sight until the wagons were unloaded and the horses fed. Then, surrounded by his 'army' he invaded the enemy's

Chapter 12: Ante Bellum Days

territory.

The Cole boys were a husky bunch of corn fed plantation Negroes, with not a coward among them. Aware of this, Jake in a truculently righteous mood, marched them militantly down the street. Seeing them coming, Jake's city tormentors sensibly took to the other side of the street. For once, they showed no aggressiveness... not even a taunting word. Smelling their fear, old Jake exultantly crossed over and blocked their path. With his boys pressing forward eagerly behind him, he began to deliberately court a ruckus. Rolling up his sleeves, he swaggered back and forth, taunting:

"Hey, dere... you lousy bunch of Babylonish Amelikites! Why for you done come ober on dis side de Jordan? Why doan you git your ol Golia an' come on down sidde de brook Cedron? Why doan you come on ober an' meet wif Saul's little David? Why doan you now?"

The city boys shifted uneasily, saying nothing... clearly wishing they were elsewhere. Waxing eloquent as more and more confidence flowed into him, Jake swung his bared arms above his head and shouted:

"How dare you come to me, you dirty Philistians, when all my disciples are a standin' about!"

They didn't dare. As one, they broke and fled. That was the end of Jake's troubles with the city hoodlums.

At some time in his life, Jake had had the misfortune to lose two fingers from his left hand. This was a matter of considerable confusion to him and one which he was particularly sensitive about.

Driving along the road one day just after a hard spring rain, he and Marse John met a colored lady who had suffered a run away with a team of oxen. The cart had been overturned and the woman spattered with mud. Coming up the road, she presented such a ludicrous spectacle that Jake,

Chapter 12: Ante Bellum Days

normally a quiet man, broke into a loud guffaw.

"Hey, dere, ole lady," he said. "You jes' been a lickin' hit, hain't ye?"

Disdaining to reply, the woman turned to Marse John and said, "Sonny, who be dat ole no-handed fool nohow?"

Feeling himself rebuked, Jake drove on, muttering, "Marse John, dat's what I specks I is...jes a old no-handed fool!"

He was always having trouble with women, in one way or the other... including Fanny. Now Fanny was a house Negro, Grandmother's maid and general helper about the house... who had also been taught the fine art of dressmaking. She was entrusted with the care of all the patterns for the clothing of the plantation Negroes. And it was she and Grandmother who saw to the making of every garment worn on that busy place. Jake had a high disdain for 'Miss Fanny', as she was generally called by the other Negroes.

"Miss Uppity Ups" is what I calls dat gal," he used to tell my father. "Jes cause she has de makin' ob my ole britches is no sign she any better what de res ob us ni***rs be nohow! You jes watch, Marse John, dat gal hain't no better'n white trash 'n someday she goin' get all mess up wid dat cantankerous proud ob her'n. Miss pooh! I tinks she done gone an' miss sore nuff already!"

When the war was over and all the Negroes were told they were free and could do as they wished, Miss Fanny was the only one of the Cole group who seemed pleased with the change. All the rest were loath to leave the plantation and the white folks who had been almost as parents to them. Soon afterward, Fanny disappeared from the plantation and no further word was heard from her.

Just before starting west, Pap and Grandma, during a trip to

Chapter 12: Ante Bellum Days

Charlottsville, were surprised to see a fine new shingle hanging out on one of the busy streets with the legend: Miss Fanny Snowball, Seamstress and Dressmaker.

Thinking to have some sewing done, Grandmother entered the place. Amazed, she discovered miss Fanny Snowball to be her erstwhile maid, Fanny!

Learning of the incident, Jake remarked, 'Allays tought dat proud ob her'n ud be gettin' de best ob dat wench. Snowball, huh! Why, Marse John, dat gal's blackerin all de res' ob us Coles put togedder! I done tol" you dat, ain't I!"

Poor old Jake! What a pity that such loyal people as he had to be turned out into a hostile world of which he had no understanding, in their old age. But since Pap could barely take care of his own, old Jake and his wives were left behind.

Years later, when Grandmother paid a visit to the old community, Jake was the most pleased of all to see her, calling himself Jake Cole and sending many words of remembrance to 'Marse John' out dere in de wes'.

As a boy, I often used to wonder if the Snowball ever got into the boiling pot... and, if so, just what was the result!

13. Some Philosophy and Other Things

The wild life of the prairies has always held a lively interest for me. And not only the wild life alone, but that of a domestic nature which must ultimately succeed in those regions. One of my saddest memories was the passing of some species of the wild to make place for another, not native to that environment.

Historically, it has been my portion to see many of the early forms, in both animal and vegetable life, give place to some other and pass from the picture forever. The buffalo, the antelope, the wild horse, the swift fox, the lobo and the grey wolf, to name a few of the larger.

As to the flora of the plains, the number and species are legion. True, their successors are of more value to the race of men who came in to possess the land when in fullness of time, it pleased God to bring about a change. But the vast agony of Nature, through the millenniums, to bring about their perfection seemed such a prodigious waste when, in a few short years of Man's sojourn, they were gone forever.

Buffalo Jones, an early day friend of my father's, must have felt the same way when he tried so desperately to secure from Congress a small tract of the Golden Range lying along Pawnee Creek for an everlasting reservation for those things.

The wild tribes have been called back from the oblivion that threatened, however they must have suffered the call. And the buffalo and antelope have yet a chance of survival. But a great number of the others are gone, never to return.

I have always felt a sort of kinship with the last of the Indian children born on the Prairies. For they must have loved and cherished the same things we white children did. The Golden Range must have been the same paradise to those children of a vanishing race as it was to us.

Chapter 13: Some Philosophy and Other Things

The same clear sky... no dust then... the same bright sun and soft prairie breeze. The mornings, so redolent of life, and the noontimes of lay indifference and the evenings so full of accomplished things.

Sometimes, I try to make myself believe that the Indians could not have sensed the change as we of a more enlightened race; that they could not pierce the future as well. Unchanged for generations, perhaps they might have had no knowledge of such things. And, hence, being ignorant may not have suffered. Yet, even as among their elders, there must surely have been some of these last children who sensed the change. And, sensing it, they, too, must have suffered in the passing of that day.

That first spring, my father built a sod house on his quarter section... moving a thousand of the little wild things to make place for himself and his family. Prairie tulips and dog-tooth violets, wild mint and prairie Pennyroyal, wild violas and buffalo peas... and a great variety of others that may never again he found in all that wide land.

The tractor and the plow and the dust of ten thousand fields have choked off their life from the land, and only their memory lingers in the minds of a few who, like me, knew and loved them.

The little stranger, who was my mother, used to gather great handfulls of the dainty passing things. Placing them in the tin tomato can, she set them in the window of the new house and pretended they were roses or honeysuckle from the garden in Missouri.

Yet she, too, knew they were a passing race and had the old scout tell her what the Indians called them. But the Indian names were very strange and hard to remember. So, thinking again of the old home in Missouri, she gave them little homey names such as wild tomato, bread root, wild sweet peas and prairie daffodils. Hyacinth and golden glow, catnip and blue bell... and various others.

Chapter 13: Some Philosophy and Other Things

The curlew, upland plover and the prairie chicken moved back across the draw when Mother would come out of the house. But they liked the shade of the soddy when the noonday sun was warm. Often, they came to cool themselves and drink from the stone trough in the yard where some hens and a noisy rooster were wont to drink. The rooster crowed, even as did his white master, and told his wild neighbors of his coming day on the prairies, and worried not at their passing.

The wolf and the lobo and the kit fox hid in the tall grass only a few yards from the soddy door and sometimes barked at the little stranger, and often at the old dog who had come so far across the miles to usurp their hunting grounds and earthen dens.

Those were passing days and my mother, just as I sensed it later, sensed it then. For her day and mine were so near one another their shadows fell often together across those early years.

When the new house was well up, a young one came to the man's den, even as the young of every kind came to the dens of the prairie in the spring time. But the baby did not tarry long on the Golden. Range... and the coyote and kit fox must move back a bit across the draw to make a place beneath the tulips for a little grave.

Seventy-five years later, we could find no spot that might be this grave, so much has the surface of the land changed.

A well was dug on the little slope that led down to the draw. There, cool, sweet water was found in abundance... and might have been used for thirsty crops had men known then what they know now. For the soil was black and rich from the roots of the grass down to the ancient sand at the water's edge.

The black colt, who had followed all across the miles... curious of all new things in this new land... must investigate this hole in the prairie

Chapter 13: Some Philosophy and Other Things

soil. As a result, he fell headlong into its gaping depth! The only means of getting the creature out was to shovel the dirt back into the hole, thus allowing it to walk out when near enough to the surface.

Those early day men had a great deal of time and patience and ingenuity, and were continually put to exercise the same. It might be the colt had a vast curiosity… or a great thirst. Four times it fell into the well before my father finally traded it off!

The stump tailed cow was sold for twenty dollars to a man who lived quite a distance from the dugout. Had it not been for the cow and the man, the Coles would have blackened their good name, possibly worse. For there came a time when, working as they might, the small wages of the men were not sufficient to bridge the gap from one pay to the next.

Hunger crept close to the soddy and dugout.

The men worked all day on the creek to get a load of wood ready for the trip to Dodge. Worked without food of any kind. The women and children could only live on hope until the men returned from town with provisions.

Three days, at least; possibly four. It could not be endured!

The store at Alexander had food, but strangers no credit.

If a man steal to satisfy his hunger, he is not condemned!

The store must be robbed… that night… of enough to satisfy until the return from Dodge.

At sundown, the stranger stopped and asked to buy the cow. Twenty dollars cash and his supper before leading her away! Eagerly, thankfully, his offer was accepted. But he must wait until Father rode into Alexander and back with provisions for supper. It being late, the stranger took the cow and went his way… and another of my family was gone.

Chapter 13: Some Philosophy and Other Things

Often, I have wondered at the prodigality of Nature on the Prairies. And paradoxically, at her wonderful economy. Although I have been able to reconcile the two I have never been able to lend but a very sympathetic ear to the voice of her passing legions. If one creature or one species must give place to another in that wonderful economy, my sympathy must always go out to the weaker. And I have wondered why it must be so.

Why worry, when the great Mother of us all may say, "I am through with you. Give way to another!"

Sufficient unto the day is the evil thereof. Also, it seems one might add: the good thereof, as well. For the Good and the Bad go down together, and tears for one might as well be tears for the other. I have grieved at the passing of the Indian, at the passing of the buffalo, at the passing of the short grass of the prairies, but I have sensed their kinship and dependence, one on the other.

The new order of the Golden Range had no need of such as they, and was only dependent until the new day be fully come.

The dirt roof on the dugout, holding down as it did the foliage of a passing generation of prairie plants made shelter in its day both new and old.

"Mr. Cole," said my Grandmother, one early spring morning. "Do you suppose there could be snakes in the roof of our house? I'm certain I heard something crawling about 'through the leaves last night'.

"Snakes in a new house!' exclaimed the old man. "Why, it was only last fall we put that roof on! Besides, you know we haven't seen a snake since we landed here."

Well, maybe I don't know much about this Golden Range of yours," she said. "But I do know one thing. There just ain't any house in the world big enough for me an' a snake at the same time!"

Chapter 13: Some Philosophy and Other Things

'Don't let it worry you, Susan," her husband said. "I can't see how there could be such a thing as a snake in there. Besides, those two pigs of ours have been runnin' around here all winter an' spring. An' pigs are poison to snakes."

Nevertheless, Grandmother was certain she heard strange sounds in the roof. In her uneasiness, she made a ceiling of old sheets, tacking them along the rafters and ridgepole in a manner to catch anything that might fall out of the overhead.

The following summer, a baby cyclone unroofed the dugout. When the men cleared out the rubbish to make way for a new roof, they killed nine large rattlesnakes!

Grandmother was scandalized. But Pap, always somewhat of a philosopher, must mention the fact that, at least, no mice or rats were found. And it is to be presumed that the pigs did their part after that, for no snakes were ever found in the new roof that went on the dugout.

14. Therapeutics of the Plains

Therapeutic knowledge on the Golden Range in those early years was as widely diffused as the homes of the settlers... and was of as great a variety of schools. Each home had its doctor and surgeon, and each of these his particular knowledge of things medical.

M.D.s were few and far between, but doctors and surgeons were another matter. Also the remedies were as abundant as the call for such things. Not always was a remedy considered in itself. The manner of its application in the various households determined its potency.

I well remember the healer who insisted on giving an infusion of roots for virtually every disease of the plains. Very carefully, he labeled each bottle with certain hieroglyphics known only to himself. Upon inquiry as to why he used the same root for each infusion, and what was the difference in the several bottles, he replied that it was all in the manner of scraping the roots.

"This bottle," he said, "contains High Cock e Lorium, and is secured by scraping the root from the big end downward. This..." indicating the other, "is Low Cock e Hirum, and is obtained by scraping from the little end upward."

Different doses and different results were obtained from the two remedies, depending on how the patient usually slept in bed... whether with high or low pillow. If no pillow was used... pillows being a luxury on the prairies... an equal dose of both infusions was given, well shaken together. This generally produced the desired result. If the patient died... well, it was just his time to go. The result would have been the same no matter how the dose had been administered.

Being only three years old at the time, my Uncle Jim was the youngest of the Cole family coming to the Golden Range in that year of

Chapter 14: Therapeutics of the Plains

1878. A very precocious youngster, Jim always managed to keep two or three of the girls busy, trying to keep him from getting into some scrape or the other.

Now Clee had an early day version of the common piggy bank, containing a number of the old one cent copper coins in use at the time. One day, to keep Jim quiet, she gave him this bank to play with. Diligent shaking and scraping failing to release any of the pennys, a crushing blow between two rocks did the job. And, lo, a handful of the huge copper coins were his to do with-as he wished.

He did what all children do. He put it in his mouth.

A considerable period of quietness out in the yard where Jim was supposed to be amusing himself. Then a sputtering and coughing that brought Grandma and Clee to the scene. A quick count of the coins showed one missing... really missing. Now the old time penny was quite some money, in size, if not in value, and not easily lost on the bare sod of the door yard. "Ma, he's swallowed it! He's swallowed one of my pennies right down his stinking little neck!"

Hastily gathering up her remaining coins, Clee retreated into the house.

"Me piggy bank, too!" gurgled the delighted youngster, pointing with one dirty finger down his throat.

Grandmother was a practical woman. But, being new on the prairies she had as yet made no contacts with the medical fraternity. Pap was away, as were the older boys. And no amount of shaking seemed to have any effect on the penny. The big coin, almost as large as a modern half dollar, had gone down without too much trouble. Possibly, Jim was indeed a prodigy!

If it would not come back up, then, Grandma reasoned, it might

Chapter 14: Therapeutics of the Plains

just go on down. And, since well oiled machinery always works the smoothest she brought forth the big bottle of castor oil in the medicine cabinet.

In those days, distance was manners on the prairies. The 'Chick Sales' of a later day not to be considered. Down over the bank of the draw 'below' for the men and 'above' for the women was all the privacy required. But woe to the female found below or the male above! In this emergency, Grandma threw tradition to the winds.

"You girls get down along the bank there," she ordered. "An' keep an eye open for that penny."

"Down where the men go, Ma?" Effie Lee exclaimed. "We girls just don't dare go down that a ways!"

"You do what I told you. Every time you see Jim go down there. You hear me! We got to get that penny through him somehow. If we don't we may have to cut him open!"

"Alright," said Effie Lee. "But Clee don't have to be so stingy with her old money nohow!"

Two days and a half along a well oiled highway and the Goddess of Liberty found herself looking into the afternoon sun, while a weary little boy trudged back to the dugout in the bank of the draw.

"It's here! It's here!" shouted Effie Lee. "I done found the penny, Ma! I done found Jim's penny!"

Her continued clamor. brought the household down along the men's side. Greedily, Clee clutched her long lost penny. "It ain't Jim's at all," she said. "An' that little buzzard ain't ever goin' to get a chance to swallow it again! I'll spend it the next time I go to Alexander. See if I don't! An' he won't get any of the candy either! So there!"

Chapter 14: Therapeutics of the Plains

Feeling himself much abused, Jim began to howl at this and would only be consoled when Grandmother promised him a big bowl of mush and milk for supper.

There were no bacteria on the prairies in those days. And it was many a year before a microbe dared show itself. Tetanus was unknown, but sometimes, we had lockjaw, which we cured by an application of well-chewed tobacco. Lacking this, fresh cow manure brought the same result. Such things as warts, wens or moles were charmed away by those versed in such occult matters.

Many a time, Pap Cole was called upon to stop bleeding, and I never heard of him losing a case. His remedy was simple. The saying of a verse from the Bible taught him by a woman. A man must learn this verse from a woman; a woman must learn it from a man. But never from man to man, nor woman to woman.

I have known of horses being ridden to death in an effort to get word to Pap of some accident on the prairie. If he was reached in time, the result was always the same. The blood stopped, and the victim recovered, be it man or beast.

This verse was never repeated aloud. Only mentally, or in an undertone. Generally, Pap would have to tell the messenger he could go, before the man realized the remedy had been applied. I once learned this verse from my Aunt Myrtle, who had it from Uncle Cass. But I was never called upon to use it.

Therapeutics were beginning to change on the prairies in my day. We had no 'appendicitis'. It is to be doubted if there was a single 'vermiform appendix' on the whole of the Golden Range at this time. But we had 'guts', both big and little, and the women folk had bowels. With the latter, a pain in those regions, if it be severe enough, was considered a case of locked bowels. In the men, it was just a plain old belly-ache, high

Chapter 14: Therapeutics of the Plains

or low... as the position of the pain might be. The remedy... castor oil in copious draughts, to the horror of modern doctors. Yet very few of us died of abdominal trouble. And the scars on our bodies were not from a surgeon's knife.

Rabies was unknown, but hydrophobia occurred when one was bitten by a mad dog or a prairie civet. At Fort Zara, on the river, was a mad-stone, the only known remedy for the condition. Sixty miles to ride, but many a cowboy did it and lived to tell the story.

Pasteur was unknown on the Golden Range, but, as I have said it was a long time before there were any bacteria there anyway.

Snake bite, we knew, for the snakes were slow in passing... and the country was not much of a pig country, at best. When bitten, we drew the poison with our lips and drank whiskey when we could get it. Few ever died from snake bite.

Bill Hass was bitten on the big toe. He tied a string around the stricken member and broke into Bert Garrett's house and filled himself with Hayner whiskey. Several hours later, he woke to find the big toe in a state of decomposition... and his head several times its wonted size. A chopping block and a sharp axe did for the toe, but it took much longer to reduce the head. Billy went back and killed the snake several days later.

Prayer was very effective, too. But it was mostly the women who prayed. The men were too busy making a living to get on speaking terms with God. Yet often the man lived because the woman prayed.

Sixty miles to the nearest town and ice... and her boy dying from pneumonia in the summer time.

"If only we had ice, we might be able to save him," sighed the Doctor, and swore because there was none.

"We'll have ice," said the determined mother. "Get down on the

Chapter 14: Therapeutics of the Plains

floor while I pray."

Ten minutes later, the prairie solitude was split by a clap of thunder… and hail piled a foot deep around the soddy!

Yes, the therapeutics of the Golden Range was much different than now, but they were effective.

Sufficient unto the day, etc. etc.

15. More Wild Flowers

The summer of '79 fulfilled Pap's prophecy of sunflower gold. For countless miles in every direction, the prairies seemed one vast sheet of burnished metal. Here was the Golden Range of his memory, and the old man seemed renewed again to the days of his youth.

The young folks, too... delighted with the golden prospect on every side... seemed to fall into his mood. Although some of them journeyed to other spots in later years, they always returned. In every sense, this land became their home.

My mother, the dreamer of the family, simply lived in a world of dreams looking upon the blooming prairie as if it had felt the touch of Midas and become an enchanted land.

The antelope played on the far ridges and were the guardian spirits of the gold on every hand. Sometimes, the wild horses raced by in great, snorting troops, scattering the antelope and coming so near the dugout she could see their bright eyes and great flowing manes and tails. And the trembling of the sod was as if an army was passing.

The colt and older work horses, disturbed by this wild life, showed a great deal more fear than the woman trembling, snorting and crowding into the doorway of the soddy until the cavalcade passed.

Sometimes, these troops left great gaping holes in the forests of gold. But soon, the warm sun and soft shower again lifted the fallen, and it was as if there had been no ravishing of the golden numbers.

The old Indian scout showed the women how these broken trees of the sunflower forest healed their wounds... pouring out, even as the pine trees, a rosin-like substance that soon covered the broken branches and bent twigs. The residue, a drop of wax-like gum, slowly hardened in the

Chapter 15: More Wild Flowers

wind.

This gum, when gathered, made a delightful chew... much like the spruce gum of Maine and Vermont. Often, the young folks of the Range used to form parties and gather the gum. Many a lifetime acquaintance was thus formed.

Mushrooms, too, sprang up among the sunflowers in untold numbers, growing always in circles on the prairies. Sometimes, the circles were as much as a mile in circumference sometimes smaller, but always the circle was there. Sometimes, the growth might be as much as a rood wide, sometimes wider, but always the circle was there.

The old scout called these circles 'buffalo stands', declaring that, in the old times, the buffalo congregated on these spots in great numbers in the summer to help one another fight the flies. Thus cultivated and enriched, the ground became a natural seed bed for the mushrooms, their spore falling in these places by countless millions. Then, becoming intermixed, they produced, through the years, the countless varieties to be found on the stands in those days.

As I have said, the scout taught my people the value of mushrooms as food. And many a splendid dinner they had, gathered from the unlimited supply continually springing up through the long summer months. There were early spring varieties late fall varieties, and summer varieties in every shape and fashion. Each family on the prairies preferred their own particular variety, deeming the countless others to be toadstools or of a poisonous nature. Personally, I doubt there was a single poisonous mushroom on the Range. I have eaten of any number of the different varieties. Only once was I the least sick. Even this instance, I think was because the mushrooms were not properly cooked.

Like the gum picking parties, people went in crowds to gather mushrooms, making a picnic of the occasion. I well remember how my

Chapter 15: More Wild Flowers

Uncle Cass's marriage brought about one of these mushroom parties. Cass had married one of the Shaben girls from over on the divide. Upon bringing her home to his new stone house, he found a group of neighbors waiting to wish them good luck.

Although being quite young at the time, I recall that Uncle Cass and his bride had little enough to eat themselves just then. So to feed the crowd of well-wishers was simply out of the question. The crowd also knew that.

"Tell you what, Cass," someone said. "This is on us. You just furnish the stove and the fire. We'll furnish the rest."

Securing an old gunny sack, some of the group set about gathering cowchips for the stove.

Grandpap Cole furnished flour for flapjacks. Hilgar Shaben, the bride's father, provided lard for frying. Someone else of the good natured crowd brought coffee and brown sugar.

The bunch divided themselves into messes; each mess large enough to fill the improvised table set up in one room. Certain women were appointed cooks, while each mess, in turn, gathered mushrooms from the surrounding prairie.

Well fried mushrooms and flapjacks! Was there aver anything so good!

We children were not allowed coffee, being given milk instead. When this failed, we went to the water barrel. (Uncle Cass was never able to bring in a well on this claim). Although it was well into the afternoon before we were served, we were well content... for we had been allowed to gather mushrooms for the others.

While doing this, some of us came upon a shallow den in the prairie sod where a mother fox had concealed her spring litter of puppies.

Chapter 15: More Wild Flowers

When the men heard about it, they took spades and shovels and, digging into the den, captured two or three of the pups.

Since prairie fox made great pets, one was given to my aunt for a wedding present. It grew into a perfect nuisance, killing the young chickens and stealing everything it could get its paws on. It soon learned its name and would come when called, much as a dog will do.

When the mushroom dinner was over, the grown folks retired to one of the largest buffalo stands. There they staged a great puff ball fight, the men against the women, using the big round mushrooms of that name much as a snow ball might be used.

My father always contended that the sunflowers were a spontaneous growth of the prairies, requiring no seed, but springing from the ground in response to a call from God Himself. This contention was due to the fact that some parts of the Golden Range would produce no sunflowers for several years in a row. Then, miraculously, so dense a growth would spring up as almost to choke the other native plants. But since this was a habit of the prairie weeds, others beside the sunflower might have been placed in the same category.

Some years, the wild onions would cover the landscape in the same manner as the sunflowers. But coming earlier, they ripened their seeds and got out of the way before the sunflower was scarcely noticeable. I have seen this brilliant member of the lily family in such numbers as to entirely crowd out every other plant but the short grass. And even this could be found only by parting the onion plants and getting down close to the ground.

Wild game could scarcely be eaten when the onion crop was good. Every thing feeding on the pungent plants became so full of the odor as to be unbearable, even when cooked. For miles around, the prairie would be a continuous flower garden of every color imaginable... A horse or cow

Chapter 15: More Wild Flowers

walking through this display of color brought forth such an odor as almost to choke anyone nearby. Milk was of no value. Even the calves had such a strong breath from nursing that one could scarce abide them.

But early summer saw the last of the onions. By this time, the sunflowers were ready to take over.

Galardia grew on the creek and river bottoms, but only in certain years. The early day farmer knew when the young of this plant showed itself in the fall, he would reap a crop of wheat the following summer. The Galardia was no pest as was the sunflower, being content with the unbroken land...and never intruding on the plowed fields.

Standing on some point of land overlooking the creek bottoms when this flower was in bloom one could see for miles up and down an unbroken ribbon of color, beautiful in the extreme... but of little value either to man or beast.

So passed the summer in a continuous riot of color. And seeing it, one could not blame the old man for calling it the Golden Range.

16. Uncle Zeke's Duel

Settlement moved westward, following the creek. Old man Harvey at Alexander, somewhere in the '60s. Later, the Youngs and the Stephens and a number of others. In 1872, J.K. Farnsworth settled in a bend almost twelve miles up the stream, on what later became the Farnsworth ranch. In '74, the Garretts, quite a family of them, took land adjoining the Farnsworth holdings. Others followed.

By the time the Coles arrived in '78, a considerable settlement had sprung up along that part of the creek. A post office was established and a small trading post named by Farnsworth for Bazine, one of Napoleon's marshals.

Joe Dixon and his brother arrived early, too. About the same time as Farnsworth. Settling down the creek about three miles from Bazine, they were one of the Coles' early day neighbors. They left the Golden Range when I was quite a small boy... somewhere around '92 or '93.

Despite my youth at the time, I can remember this family quite well. Especially the boys, some of whom were near my own age. Old Joe, as he was usually called, had come while there were buffalo yet to be had and he still had quite a number of buffalo robes around his house. He was a great wildhorse man, too. He brought in many a herd to his creek ranch, taming and selling them to the settlers and to the few other established places in the country.

On the south side of the creek, just above the Dixon place was a family of old timers by the name of Long. Ezekial Long. Uncle Zeke, everybody, called him. Although I do not remember the day of his coming, my earliest recollections must always include Uncle Zeke and his large family of boys and girls. A historian need only select any one of the numerous families, and that family's history must necessarily be a history

Chapter 16: Uncle Zeke's Duel

of the entire country, so closely were our fortunes interwoven.

Uncle Zeke was a little man, not over five feet six, wearing a short grey beard and moustache and hair a little on the careless order. Most men wore their hair long in those days. Barbers were few and far between on the Golden Range in 1876, and even later. A haircut was to be had only at the hands of some prairie wife wielding the family scissors.

Only 'Crazy Ed' knew much about sharpening scissors. 'Crazy Ed' ranged anywhere from Fort Worth on the south to Deadwood on the north. From Leavenworth on the east to Sante Fe on the west. Since his going and coming was always on foot, the scissors were sometimes a bit dull by the time he arrived.

Maybe that was why the men, including Uncle Zeke always wore beards and moustaches and let their hair grow long.

Uncle Zeke gave one the idea of being extremely old, and I suppose he must have been. For the Long boys and girls I knew were part of the second family he had raised.

He was the only Mexican War veteran, other than my grandfather, living on that part of the Golden Range. He and my grandfather are also the only two from that war buried at Bazine.

If Uncle Zeke seemed very old he was also very wise. Not so much in book learning, but in a great fund of homey wisdom that made him a man of much service and reputation in a new country like the Golden Range. Always ready to help in anything pertaining to the community good... or ready to give advice on any subject that might come up... he was loved and respected by all who knew him.

One day, in the days of her boom, a smart aleck lawyer came to the new town of Bazine. Being a stranger, he did not, of course, know Uncle Zeke, nor the old man's wisdom. Neither did he have any idea of

Chapter 16: Uncle Zeke's Duel

the respect in which Uncle Zeke was held by the entire neighborhood. Probably, it wouldn't have made any difference. As I have said, he was a smart aleck.

One Saturday afternoon, this character put in most of his time teasing Uncle Zeke's oldest son George, a gawky country lad about fifteen years old. He found it very amusing, this smart aleck, and his friends.

Now George, while not too bright, had inherited quite a bit of Uncle Zeke's native wisdom. In the course of the afternoon, he managed to give a pretty good account of himself. However, his quaint, proverbial manner of accomplishing this only provoked his tormentors to higher glee.

Uncle Zeke, feeling, I presume, that George was able to take care of himself, said nothing.

Late in the evening, George withdrew from the crowd and began quietly whittling on a bit of pine board. The lawyer, unable to let well enough alone, approached him and proposed a knife trade. Now a knife being a necessity on the prairies, and everybody carrying one, a knife trade was not out of order. So when asked by the lawyer how he would trade, George hesitated... wondering whether the man was in earnest.

"I dunno," he said finally. "Let's see your knife."

Closing his own, he passed it to the lawyer for inspection. Just a piece of knife it was, such as boys usually have. One broken blade and a piece of handle on one side.

On the other hand, the lawyer's knife, tendered for his inspection, was a grand new affair. Three blades and a corkscrew with mother of pearl handles and a silver name plate on the side.

Watching the look of wonder and surprise on the boy's face, the lawyer and his friends snickered behind their hands. The simple fool!

Chapter 16: Uncle Zeke's Duel

George said nothing for a moment. He just sat there, carefully inspecting the beautiful implement, stroking the pearly sides... now and then catching a glimpse of his own face reflected in the name plate. Opening the shining new blades, he felt their edges and tested their strength.

"Well," he said at last. "I guess we'll call it a trade," and slipped the knife in his pocket.

Taken off guard, the lawyer said hastily, "Just a minute, boy. That's a fine new knife. You'll have to pay some boot."

"A trade's a trade," the boy said stubbornly. "Besides, you didn't say nothin' about boot. Should a said so to begin with. It's too late now. The knife's mine."

The crowd who had witnessed the deal roared with laughter. Ridicule was something the lawyer couldn't take. Angrily, he grabbed the boy, demanding, "You country yokel! Give me back that knife!"

Uncle Zeke, who had been a quiet witness to the affair, moved in between the lawyer and George.

"Leave the boy alone," he said quietly.

"You keep out of this!" his face dark with anger, the lawyer whirled on the old man. "Just who in the hell do you think you are anyway!"

"I happen to be the boy's father," Zeke said, his voice taking on a perceptible chill. "But I'd a stepped in, no matter who the boy. 'As a dog turneth again to his vomit, so doth a fool to his folly!' That fits you pretty well, Mister. You've been having a lot of fun all afternoon at this simple boy's expense. You couldn't leave him alone when he went off to whittle by himself. No; you had to come back for more. Well, you got just what was coming to you. Now, I mean you shall leave the boy alone."

Chapter 16: Uncle Zeke's Duel

Had the lawyer been anything but what he was, he would have heeded the old man's warning. Instead, to make a great show, he challenged Uncle Zeke to a duel.

Immediately, several of the bystanders protested. "Leave him alone! He's a fine, respected man. We'd have a hard time getting along without him."

"Yeah. An' be warned, fellow. Any harm comes to Uncle Zeke the country will hold you responsible."

"You're a smart man. Can't you see the boy's a little simple. He didn't mean no harm."

But the more they talked, the more determined the lawyer, the more insulting his talk and manner toward the old man. Finally, seeing nothing else would satisfy the man, Uncle Zeke agreed to give him satisfaction.

"We knew Uncle Zeke was no coward," said my father, in telling of the event afterward. "But we knew he didn't have a chance. It was well rumored that the lawyer was an expert with most any of the weapons then in use on the prairies. So, as a personal friend of Zeke's, I went to him and begged him not to be so rash."

"It's all right, John, it's all right," Zeke said. "I don't think anybody's goin' to get hurt very badly. Now, I'll be obliged if you'll act as my second."

Being the man challenged, Uncle Zeke had the choice of weapons. But, for some reason, he refused to name them, insisting that the weapons would be furnished by himself at the proper time. He insisted that the duel be fought at sun-up on his ranch down the creek. Also, the fight was to be kept secret., he not wishing his women folk to know about it until it was over.

Chapter 16: Uncle Zeke's Duel

Day break found a large crowd assembled out near the barn on the Long ranch. A murmur rose as Uncle Zeke walked from the house, barefooted and wearing only a pair of belt overalls.

One again, my father sought to dissuade the old man, for his family's sake, to abandon the fight. But Zeke seemed not in the least disturbed.

"John, I've lived a long time in the land," he said. "And I've never yet seen the righteous forsaken nor his seed begging bread."

The lawyer, more excitable, kept insisting that the shooting irons... or whatever weapons Zeke had chosen... be produced at once. His seconds wanted to examine them. The doctor, too, wished to know just what kind of wounds he might have to treat.

Lest his women folk be disturbed, Uncle Zeke led the company out behind the barn... and to a large corral full of drowsy cattle. Opening the corral gate, the old man drove the cattle out onto the prairie. Then, turning to the tense, waiting crowd he said calmly:

"Gentlemen, I have chosen the weapons with which to fight this duel. And, now, if my opponent is ready..."

"The weapons, sir, the weapons!" the lawyer demanded impatiently. "Enough of this nonsense!"

"Why, the weapons, counselor," Uncle Zeke replied mildly. "Here right under your feet. All the green cow manure you can throw!"

"That lawyer didn't want to fight half as bad as he thought he did," my father laughed, in telling about it afterward. "He made himself scarce around the Long ranch in short order. In high good humor, Zeke had the rest of us down to the house for breakfast."

17. Philosophy, Hodgepodge, and 'Bunker Hill'

Faith is ever stronger than reason, and much more satisfying.

Looking back over nearly eighty years, the people and events of those days seem shadowy and unreal. And when I try to recall them, they slip away... and reason is hard put to bring them again to momentary existence. For faith is the substance of things hoped for, and the evidence of things not seen.

Walking from the homestead to the creek across the Walnut bottoms that first summer, my father stopped for a moment where Highway 96 now crosses those level lands.

"Someday, Tilly," he said "We will see a railroad running right along here."

The railroad came, but the man who visualized it and the man who built it are no more. Reason asks if aver they existed. And the faith that called for the railroad, and the countless other things they builded, seems shadowy and unreal.

What is it they have done, these men of another day? We no longer need the railroad nor but very few of the things they dreamed of and hoped for. Their vision, fulfilled, would be most unsatisfying to them... were they here to view it. Sufficient unto the day the evil thereof. And the good, too, we might add.

With a prophetic spirit I looked upon those things as a boy, and realized that, so far as I was concerned, never in all the history of the world, in time nor eternity, would there ever again be such days, such people and such hopes.

The things we wanted then, men of today would not want. They have no need desire for them. Even the topography of the land is changed.

Chapter 17: Philosophy, Hodgepodge, and 'Bunker Hill'

And when I would tell of how it was in those days, men turn away, uninterested.

Yet God must have been well pleased with the Golden Range as it was when I first looked upon it. For, in a million years, He had asked for no change, and, I am constrained to believe, would have asked for none in a million more had He been questioned in the matter.

From oxcart to aeroplane in a single generation! From ten miles per day to ten thousand! The earth no place for a single natural thing.

Pap Cole looked down the years and saw the fields ripe to the harvest and said:

"Some day this whole country will be one great field of wheat."

But it wasn't wheat that brought him to the Golden Range, nor the hope of wheat... but a desire to escape those things and find a land new from the hand of God. It wasn't the railroad nor the hope of the railroad that made my father sing Home on the Range the first thing of a morning... but the wild, free beauty on every side and the voice of God coming up from the south.

Truly, they sowed and others have reaped. But the increase has not been in material things. The real wealth of the Golden Range is not in bushels of wheat nor miles of railroad, but in the golden dreams of a contented people.

A few years, Pap lived in the soddy and the dugout in the bank of the draw. Then he sold the claim to a newcomer and moved on up the creek a little, near to the new town.

By this time, Jenny had captured her native', and most of the young people were growing up. My sister and I had come to my father's house. Then, shortly after, another brother and another. Eight of us lived to grow up... five girls and three boys, all of us well and happy.

Chapter 17: Philosophy, Hodgepodge, and 'Bunker Hill'

In those early years, my father and grandfather ranched together. My happiest recollection is holding on to the back of a saddle behind my Uncle Jim (he of the 'penny' fame) while we herded the great droves of cattle they had managed to get together.

An almost equally happy incident was the acquisition of my first suit of Sunday clothes during this same period. Made from Army blue, it was bought for a trifle on one of my father's numerous trips to the fort at Hays. Grandmother spent several days cleaning the discarded uniform and cutting it down to fit a boy of five. Proudly donning my new suit and, with a soldier's cap to match, I went out into the yard to show it to Pap.

The old man, with a merry twinkle in his eyes, would deign me no recognition, but muttered, "Damn Yankee!" under his breath... and made as if to strike me with his cane.

Men came to trade horses with my father, but, usually only once. If they returned a second time, my father became suspicious and put on his 'trading clothes' as he expressed it. None that I recall ever returned a third time. Except Wiley Cloustan... and, of course, he was different. Being from Virginia, he and Father were the best of friends.

Wiley owned a big horse ranch several miles up the creek where he kept a string of breeding stock... horses and Jacks. Since Wiley wanted mules for an eastern market and Father had a big bunch of mares, business was good. Sixty dollars per head at weaning time, plus the service fee for every mule colt. Money came easy in those days!

Wiley was the one man who always came back for more. He and Father were continually trading, each trying, in a friendly fashion to beat the other. The loser always accepted his defeat with a wry good humor, there being no room for rancor, in their natures.

One of these 'battle of wits' is unforgettable. Father had traded for

Chapter 17: Philosophy, Hodgepodge, and 'Bunker Hill'

a bunch of range stock, among which was a beautiful bay mare. Unfortunately, she was a loco... a horse addicted to the Loco weed... and not to be depended upon. Although the mare showed no signs of being an addict, she was, for all her beauty, virtually worthless.

Immediately upon securing her, my Father naturally (out of the goodness of his heart, of course!) thought of his friend Wiley. Such a beautiful mare, he told himself, would surely be an asset to the Clouston ranch. Wiley simply must have her. So…

Casually, Father drove down the road past the Clouston house. Tied alongside the team, the beautiful mare trotted with graceful rhythm, her dainty head high. Apparently anxious to get home, Father showed no intention of stopping, pushing the team forward at a brisk clip.

Now curiosity was Wiley's weakness, especially where a splendid looking mare was concerned. He wasted no time. Soon the passing wagon was in the Clouston barnyard and the two friends were hard at it making a deal. Although Wiley brought forth several splendid animals, Father pointed out that he already had about all the horses he could handle. A trade was out of the question. Money would be the only consideration and, actually, he wasn't too anxious about that. After all, the mare looked and acted like a mule mare; a colt or two from her would be worth more than the paltry one hundred dollars he was asking for the beautiful creature. Besides, he was in considerable of a hurry. He had to get going.

Wiley capitulated.

"Alright! Tie her to the back of that wagon," he said. "and come on in the house while I write you a check. She just ain't worth that much money, but we're goin' to trade anyway."

'Bunker Hill' proved to be his second mistake.

Now, 'Bunker Hill' was a flea-bitten roan of doubtful lineage and

Chapter 17: Philosophy, Hodgepodge, and 'Bunker Hill'

even more doubtful age, who had been wished off on Father in one of his numerous horse trades. Balky, with a disinclination to work, Bunker Hill was not only an obstinate creature but, worse, at some time in his life he had taken to the weed... as the saying went on the prairies.

Absolutely valueless, the horse had a personality unique among his kind. He had been known to try the patience of men far less devout than Billy Walknitz, and men who were far better horsemen.

Having no particular need for the animal, Father had put him out on wheat pasture for the winter. There he seemingly forgot all about his late evil habits. He even proceeded to take on a fine new coat of hair and an old age spread that made him look quite a horse. Perhaps, just to help the good work along, he got a dose or two of antimony as well. (Father was quite a veterinary in his day, as well as a fine rider.)

With the coming of spring, the stock had to be removed from the wheat, so Bunker Hill was brought home to the barn. At this time, Father was in charge of the only livery stable and sale stable in town. Hence, Bunker Hill had the run of the vacant lots around this place. As might be expected, he soon made friends, with the horses of the Walknitz team, they having the same priviledge of the lots every Sunday. On this one day, we boys were permitted to ride the flea-bitten roan, but only when he was in a good humor.

Early one Monday morning, neighbor Walknitz called across the fence to my Father. "John, I stand in need of a good big horse this spring to take care of my work. That 'Ni***r' of mine is a bit light for a work horse. If I could replace him with something a bit heavier, it would suit me well."

Now 'Ni***r' was a clean limbed pony that some of the boys in the community swore could do a quarter mile in a pretty short time. In fact, they had given the pony a tryout one night with some of the fastest horses

Chapter 17: Philosophy, Hodgepodge, and 'Bunker Hill'

in the vicinity. All this unbeknown to Billy, of course.

Father had been commissioned to secure the horse if possible, but, knowing Billy's Methodist inclinations had hesitated to approach him concerning the horse.

"I just wonder, John," continued the would-be trader, "if you would give me a good neighborly trade? Not any of your horse jockey stuff, but a real neighborly trade. Just like one neighbor with another."

"Well, Billy," said Father. "I suppose we might trade if I had anything like a work horse that I could recommend. But I just haven't got a thing on hand right now that you would want; not a single thing."

"Now I don't know about that, John," said Billy. "How about that Bunker Hill horse the boys have been riding around here? He seems about the right size, and I like his looks pretty well."

Thou shalt not covet. Not thy neighbor's ox, nor his ass. Nor his Bunker Hill, neither!

"Oh, no, Billy! You don't want Bunker Hill. He just wouldn't suit you at all."

"Listen, John." A determined note crept into Billy's voice. "I asked for a good neighborly horse trade, not any of your jockeying. Just as one neighbor to another. I want to trade you my Ni***r for your Bunker Hill. Of course, Bunker Hill is a little bigger than my horse, but I'm willing to pay the difference."

Where was the guardian angel of the innocent that spring morning!

"Now, come on, John! Just a good neighborly trade." It was Billy's second offense, and, as Father used to say, "He was of age."

Fifteen dollars to boot between the black pony and the venerable Bunker Hill!

Chapter 17: Philosophy, Hodgepodge, and 'Bunker Hill'

We boys could work him when he was in the mood, but Billy never understood the moods of a balky horse.

Bunker Hill went back to his grazing in the alleys, while Ni***r graduated into the best quarter horse in the community!

18. About the Night

Night on the prairies was an unforgettable experience. A different wonder to that of the morning, it stole over one like a great benediction. The soul was lifted toward the Infinite, and one became God-conscious whether he would or not.

The mornings offered so much in the way of life that one became infatuated with living before the sun was scarcely up. But when the great shadows of the world stretched themselves languidly across the Universe... when the winds died down and the tired leaves of the grass fluttered to repose and the little wild things began their vesper song... then the soul could not help but know that God was very near.

Earthly values faded on the prairies in the evening. There was more wealth in the memory of deeds well done than in the gold of Midas. The plaintive mooing of the homing herd granted a satisfaction no conqueror could ever know.

It was then the shadows came in from the outermost reaches of Time, stealing away the treasures of the day. And before one had time to make them secure, their substance was repudiated. But the night had a value and a treasure all its own. One was well repaid for the theft of daylight things in a coin that must have been minted in a celestial land, so different was the seal and superscription.

When the sun was well settled in the sea of grass, and the shadows of the ant hills stretched themselves to nothingness in the gulf of darkness coming up out of the east... when every thing of the day had withdrawn into the canyons of memory and only the pinnacles of darkness towered over-head... then came the ghost of the dead day, to chide, to chide for the unaccomplished.

Could we have had again the doing, as we had but a few short hours

Chapter 18: About the Night

before, how different would the tale have been told! But the day was dead forever, and no manner of remorse could restore the privilege that was ours at the morning... or even at the dreamy half way of noon when, for a moment, we made resolve to do double stint.

Gone were all the grand cloud shapes, the fair cities we built, the great countries we claimed, even the fallow fields we were to have planted. (Never is the accomplished equal to the vision!) The shadows caught away the dream shapes and, for the moment, one felt naked and alone. Like the little prairie wolf, if one could have done so, one would have given way to the melancholy and cried for the departed day to return again.

Although it was summertime and one needed no coat, the breath of night seemed to bear a chill that came surely from the corpse of the dead day. One shivered lest the ghost confront one in the half light that still remained. Could one have remembered some sanctuary, how gladly he would have retreated therein, leaving the remorse of the day behind.

From where we stood, a golden pathway led into the mystic west and into the departed day. We determined to follow and gather our robes about us, half heartedly, but again procrastination despoiled us. And while we loitered, the pathway was loosed from either end, and as a scroll, was rolled up by a giant hand and placed in the limbo of forgotten things.

Thus, naked and alone, the night found us and, wrapping her robe around us, bade us be of good cheer.

The chill was gone, and gone the senseless grieving for the lost day. The sentinel stars came out, taking their place in the fair fields of heaven. The east was no longer a place of shadows, but a door, slightly ajar. Out there, somewhere, was morning and a new day.

But we did not worry. The night that was upon us would surely purge us of the old evil... and the purging would be like a soothing

Chapter 18: About the Night

ointment. We would go out under the stars and, counting them one by one, we would hang the cares that had beset us throughout the day upon their shining points. When the new day came, they would be carried into that oblivion where the stars go when the night is done.

Beautiful, patient, peaceful Mother Night! The night that came so tranquilly, so majestically over the prairie lands of the Golden Range.

Even in our everyday living, it seemed to play a vital part. Uncle Gil had a claim upon which he must stay at least one night in every six months... or lose his right to a patent from Uncle Sam. On the highest point, he built a little frame shack, but the wild horses and roving herds of cattle soon rubbed it down and the cyclones scattered it abroad. Still, every six months he managed to sleep one night somewhere on the one hundred and sixty acres. Each time he always managed to have a witness to the fact.

Why one night? Why would not the day alone suffice? Because the night was made for a oneness the day could not accomplish. One must sleep with the land to really understand it. Nor could any amount of daylight bind as did the soft embrace of night. Like a new wife, one must take this gift of Uncle Sam's in his arms and lie down on the connubial bed and spend a night there to be really wedded. But once one has slept there, he will be loath to leave.

As Billy the Kid once said: "This is my country, New Mexico. There just ain't officers enough in the whole United States to run me out."

So also with the Golden Range, and those who came to know it.

Since my Uncle never found water shallow enough to dig a well to, we always took a jute sack of water and cold food the nights I spent with him on the claim. Supper and breakfast we ate there, and were satisfied. Why shouldn't Uncle Sam be? Evidently he was, for my Uncle

Chapter 18: About the Night

was eventually granted a patent to the land.

Personally, I am convinced that no claim was ever proven up that the claimant did not spend at least one night thereon.

Like the Bible story, it takes the evening and the morning to make the day. The soft tranquility of the evening, after supper, and the gentle homing sounds of the wild things as they settled down to rest, just naturally made one feel he was a part of the land.

We had our saddle blankets for cover, the soft green grass for a mattress and 'the stars for tapers tall'. As we lay there on the prairie my Uncle would tell me about the heavens... while I stared fascinated, up at the stars. Stars by the countless millions, all of them seeming so terribly near. Often I used to reach my hand out from under the saddle blanket and try to touch the nearer ones. I went to sleep with the evening star and woke with the morning star... the sweet, rancid smell of sweaty saddle blanket and prairie pennyroyal in my nostrils. Little wonder that I became wedded to the prairies in a manner no power on earth can break.

My cousin, John Bailey's grandma came out from Missouri to spend the summer with her son, my Uncle Bill. While on the prairies, she tried to teach us boys the wonders of astronomy. John always swore his grandma was the smartest woman who ever lived, declaring she knew the exact number of stars in the entire universe, most of which she could point out and call by name. However that might be, she had evidently had a course in astronomy at some time in her life. She told us many things we had never dreamed of, making our prairie sky at night a place of fascination and wonder.

Many of the constellations we learned by name and were able to point out. Also when we might expect them... and in just what part of the heavens they might be found at the different seasons of the year. Once we learned to tell the time of night by the position of the Big Dipper, it would

Chapter 18: About the Night

have been a difficult matter to lose one of us on a starry night. In fact, never once did I know the sensation of being lost in all the years I lived on the Golden Range.

It took a visit to Missouri for that experience...and in only sixteen acres of timber!

God seemed so terribly near on the prairies at night. Perhaps because, like one at prayer, every other thing was shut out, leaving God and me alone.

Very few crimes were committed on the Range at night, the outlaw preferring to sleep then and wait for the light of day to do his work. At night one could not tell the color of an adversary's eyes, a mistake could be made so easily. In the big city, this was different. There the night had already been turned into day. No city dweller ever knew the tranquility of the night.

My uncle taught me early to take my bed out on the prairie and away from roads and buildings. We were not afraid of spooks. But a house, especially an abandoned one, might conceal some unwelcome visitor to the Range. Occasionally, bad men from the cities came west. Generally, we found them in some such place, especially at night. Prairie men, therefore, avoided these places, making their beds with only the starry sky for a roof.

Even in a storm, we much preferred the wide open to the hampering confusion of strange walls. The voices of the night were not for him who slept beneath a roof. And if he be a bit superstitious, strange walls only added to his affliction.

Tranquility and peace of mind came alone from God and, to sense these in their fullness, one must sleep on the prairies. Be the night calm or otherwise, the Great Spirit was there, and 'He spoke a various language.'

Chapter 18: About the Night

The same voice was not heard beneath man-made roofs nor behind man-made walls. Those who sought God went forth beneath the stars and listened to His words. The soul was-renewed, and the same voice was in the storm and in the calm.

A good tarpaulin, a pair of blankets, the prairie sod... these and a starry night. Me and my God.

19. Life, Cattle, Sheep - and Jim

Life is one grand adventure in living. And if one begins that adventure as we did on the Golden Range... with the very first day of life and the very early morning of that day... then, when the last days come, the evening will find him ready for the shadows.

Knowing what I do now about life, I would not care to repeat the adventure. But then that is because I have seen the end insofar as the world and myself are concerned. However, if the Cosmonaut who finally bridges the light years of space to some other universe would only take me along, how gladly would I renew the adventure of living!

Somehow, I am unable to stir up much enthusiasm over plain, every day life in the near future. I have never been very much in sympathy with any deal that might be bought with money or with some other fellow's consent. I have always liked the morning better than any other part of the day, and always liked to get up and get going before the other fellow knew what I was about. Later, if he felt like it, he could throw in and go along with me as long as he was in a congenial mood. But I never liked to be told how far I could go by anyone... either by a single man or by society.

On the Golden Range we knew very little about license. For a considerable period, I questioned the advisability of securing a license to marry. Probably had I not had a very persuasive partner in the venture I would have avoided it entirely. In my father's day, they had no such things as marriage licenses, and it always seemed like a mercenary thing to me when the custom became fashionable. Now one must have a license to justify virtually anything one does. It seems to me this has robbed us of much of the adventure of living.

When I think of Life, I sense the dewey freshness of the mornings that came to us on the prairies. And, instinctively, I look about for my

Chapter 19: Life, Cattle, Sheep - and Jim

saddle and bridle and wonder where the horse is.

Oh, give me a home where the buffalo roam, Where the deer and antelope play,

Where seldom is heard a discouraging word, And the skies are not clouded all day.

Never a Morning passed that my father did not sing a few lines of that beautiful old range song. And certainly, my days were made more wonderful by the hearing of it. Personally, I much prefer the snort of a good horse to the purr of the best automobile ever built. We lived as we went along. Now one has to go along... and at a nerve-racking pace... if he would live at all.

As a boy, I received most of my education, both in the art of living and working, at the hands of my Uncle Jim. He taught me almost everything I know about cattle and horses and all the animals of the range as well as most of the plants. He had a name for them all, and a reason for everything they did. Why they grew this way or why that, and what would have been the result had they done otherwise.

Socially, he knew every rancher and his wife and children in a hundred mile radius. From a boy's point of view, he possessed even more practical knowledge. For instance, where every melon patch was planted and when the first ripe fruit could be expected to appear. Which one of the numerous neighbors might well shoot anyone caught in his melon patch and which had a vicious dog. Moreover, he was generally familiar with the locks on most of the dugouts and soddies, if any were used. I firmly believe that had my Uncle Jim been born in the days of such things, he would have been a pirate bold, driving his galleon against the shipping of the world!

In more ethical fields, his knowledge was also considerable. He

Chapter 19: Life, Cattle, Sheep - and Jim

taught me about the stars at night and the storms by day... and many the gales we weathered together, both in winter and summer. I learned how to fight prairie fires alongside him. And how to get a drink from a crawfish hole in the dry draws of a summer drought.

History was ever-ready at his tongue's end; time and again, he fought most of the battles of the Revolution and Civil War for my enlightenment. He knew all about the different weapons used, and even how to load and cock a cannon. One huge piece of ordinance he used to tell me about was "so big it took a yoke of oxen to pull the ball into place in the barrel." When I innocently inquired how they got the oxen out again before firing the cannon, he called me a dummy and said they "drove them out the touch hole, or course!"

Through Uncle Jim I became acquainted with George Washington and his little hatchet. Later, he told me all about Adam and Eve and their two sons and taught me a little rhyme that went something like this:

"Adam was the first man,

Eve was t'other.

Cain was a bad man

'cause he killed his brother."

One morning we went to old man Park's dugout to Sunday School. When the responsive reading was read, I jumped off my seat and repeated this little rhyme to the consternation of my mother and the huge satisfaction of my instructor.

According to Uncle Jim, the Devil lived underground and was constantly on the lookout for girls. However, he would also sometimes pick up small boys who got in his way or, in any manner, acted 'sissy'. To avoid his Satanic Majesty, one had to know all about girls; hence, I was early instructed in those mysteries. Babies, I was told, had nothing to do

Chapter 19: Life, Cattle, Sheep - and Jim

with a stork, but came to their mothers in much the same manner as the calves and colts with which we were familiar.

Santa Claus was a huge joke and looked so much like Pap one couldn't tell the difference.

Women all went to heaven when they died; most of the men went to hell. Only Pap and John had any chance of escape, and there were grave doubts about John.

A coward was a thing to be despised, and a thief, as well, if he was caught.

A dry land tortoise, of which there were plenty on the prairies, was the earthly impersonation of Satan. We always rode far around one of these if we happened to meet him in the road.

One day when I was riding with Jim and Andy Wolfe, they had to ride off hell-bent-far-leather to keep their cattle from some fellow's kaffir field. Since I was riding double with Jim, he said, "Slide down, boy! We got to hurry! We'll bring the cattle back to the old Conant house. You meet us there."

As I hit the ground, they were on their way, riding hard. A quarter mile up the road Andy deliberately dropped his lunch sack because it was getting in his way. Naturally, he expected me to pick it up and bring it with me to the old house. But that particular day my imagination was very vivid. Approaching the sack, I saw, not Andy's lunch... but the Devil sticking his head up out of the ground. He wasn't going to fool me! Taking a wide circle around, I reached the house safely but empty handed. His Satanic Majesty didn't have a ghost of a chance with me in those days... so well had I been tutored in his ways!

But if I was a pretty good match for the Devil, I was a sorry match for a more earthly opponent. Sometimes I still flush when I think of the

Chapter 19: Life, Cattle, Sheep - and Jim

incident. A simple visit with my mother and sister to Andree Forbes' photo shop for a tintype. That was all. And yet I wet my new pants and stared, my eyes bugged out in a frightful manner, as the photographer aimed his cannon at me! Only by reminding myself that a coward was not to be tolerated in the Cole family was I able to get through the ordeal. My sister still has the tintype. It is dramatic evidence of my fright!

Now and then, Jim got himself into trouble... like the time a certain Dutchman got his entire herd while he was fishing. The Dutchman demanded twenty dollars damage to his crops by the herd. Either Jim paid on the spot or went home without his cattle. But he remembered that Pap had a great quantity of Confederate money, brought from Virginia after the war. And Pap had said he would be away most of the day.

Smiling, Jim swung into his saddle. "Stick around," he told the Dutchman, and headed across the fifteen miles of prairie to the ranch. Digging down into Pap's old trunk, he filched a Confederate twenty dollar bill... not worth the paper it was printed on... and rode back to the Dutchman's place. The Dutchman, never having seen a Confederate bill, accepted it without question. Jim took his cattle and went home. The next day, a badly confused Dutchman tried unsuccessfully to spend the twenty at Lacross... after a long thirty mile ride! Madder than hell, he tried to have Jim pinched for counterfeiting... with an equal lack of success!

Pap never missed the twenty dollar bill.

Around that time, a great fad for collecting candy hearts swept the prairies. Candy hearts of every kind and description, big, little and indifferent. Now Jim liked candy hearts, so did I. So did Bill Emily, a would-be fiddler. The three of us put our heads together and quickly came up with a logical solution to our problem.

Cad Bunting, a newly-wed living in a dugout on the range, offered wonderful possibilities. Or, more truthfully, his wife did. It was well

Chapter 19: Life, Cattle, Sheep - and Jim

known that she had a splendid collection of candy hearts. Just how Jim and Bill knew Cad and his wife were away from home that particular day, I don't know. But they obviously did, for we rode boldly up to the dugout and, without waste of time removed the single sash from the window. (As I said, Jim was quite skilled in such matters!) Both Jim and Bill wriggled inside. In moments, a big box of candy hearts was passed out, along with Cad's fiddle and bent willow bow.

While Jim continued his search for more candy, Bill sat in the shade of the dugout, 'fiddlin' with the fiddle'. The most plaintive music I ever heard kept rising and falling on the summer air. l Suddenly, a clatter of hooves came beating down over the hill! Jumping to his feet, Bill pitched the fiddle through the window. Jim busted out with another box of candy hearts under his arm. The three of us scuttled away and hid in the cane field nearby.

The pounding of hooves swept past, faded away into the distance. We rose and stood grinning sheepishly at one another. It was only a wild horse racing across the land.

"Better go back an' have another look," Jim said. "Might have missed some. An' I sure got a sweet tooth!"

Such a man was my Uncle Jim!

20. Wild Horses and Wilder Men

The wild horse was the last of the larger wild animals to disappear from the Golden Range. Actually, his was not so much a disappearance, as a gradual amalgamation with the tamer stock of the settlers. A change brought about almost completely by the wild horse hunters of the Range.

In the '80s, these wild-horse-men were numerous in our neighborhood. Saint Rowe; Bill Keuffer, Wild Horse Bill, Doc Tichnour, Jake Kaufman, the Garret boys, Joe Dickson, old man Herd and dozens of others. These were the heroes of my dream days, the days when the wild horse was passing from the Golden Range.

Up the creek from the first dugout on the claims, certain of these wild-horse men built a circular stone corral, enclosing almost ten acres of ground. Many a wild drove I have watched brought in from farther west by these men, as wild as the horses they brought in. Once the herd was stampeded into the corral and the gate closed behind it, word went out that horses were for sale. Immediately, settlers came from far and wide to trade for the much needed stock.

Wild horses were not as hard to tame as one might think, and, once tamed, made excellent work stock... both for saddle and harness. Since the wild-horse men were generally required to catch and saddle the horse for the buyer, we had a rodeo there at the old stone corral every time a wild bunch was brought in: Sometimes, they were also required to ride the animal at least once before the buyer would take it easy.

Just who first built this corral above the claims, I am not sure. However, my father took me with him at different times to look over some herd that had been driven in.

One spring morning when I was only three years old, my father and mother went to visit a man named Buck Couch who lived near the old

Chapter 20: Wild Horses and Wilder Men

corral in the very early times... along with his wife, one daughter and several large boys.

Although there was quite a number of wild stallions in the corral that morning, we only climbed up on the fence to take a look at them. Some of those stallions were quite vicious, with their wicked, yellow teeth and deadly, slashing hoofs. One did well to keep away from them, which we did.

From the conversation between Couch and my father, I am certain Couch and his boys had something to do with the horses in the corral. Either they had brought them in, or helped to do so. Horse thieves later stole some fine horses from this man, Couch. He and his boys followed them all the way to Dodge where they found and claimed the horses. The thieves, however, escaped into Indian country south of Dodge.

Later, after Dad and Couch had finished talking, we went for a walk up along the hillside. It was springtime. The slopes were one great flower garden as far as one could see up and down the creek. I remember distinctly wanting to pick a certain sturdy flower blooming there, but could not because the stem was so tough I could not break it. One of the Couch boys, a big, fine looking chap, pulled out his jack-knife and cut the stem for me and I bore the flower to the house in triumph. The Couch boy called it a Ni***r Head, but I later learned it was the flower of the prairie snake root or Aconita, which the old timers used to dig and sell to drug men.

In looking back over those early years, that one morning stands out with such beauty, such grandeur, so much of the wild, free glory of just living, it would be worth a lifetime of prosaic days to have lived its few poetic hours. Certainly the wild horses, charging back and forth across the corral in their fright, were a thrilling part of the wonders that made up the day. So, too, was that one flower.

Even now, when I think of wild horses, I sense a sparkling

Chapter 20: Wild Horses and Wilder Men

morning, a flowery hillside, a man who was my father, a big, fine looking boy in frontier clothing and a little boy with a snake root blossom in his hand. And there is still the scent of the morning, with the flowers on every side, the sweaty odor of my father's hair as he lifted me and my Aconita blossom to his shoulder, the soft, pungent horsey smell of the corral... It is good to have lived that day! Good to have lived in the day of the wild horse and the wilder men who hunted them.

No account of wild horse hunting would be complete without mentioning the art of 'creasing' a horse in order to capture a herd. Now creasing took considerable skill with a rifle. One had to place a bullet through the neck, just behind the ears and close to the neck bone. A well placed shot would bring the animal down, paralyzing it for a short time... thus enabling the hunter to secure it with rope or hobble. Usually, no serious effects resulted, the horse regaining full use of its powers.

In creasing, however, many a good horse was killed by a poor shot. But even if the leader was killed, the herd was soon brought under control, becoming confused without the dead leader. And one horse made little difference to the horse men... not when there were millions roaming the prairies.

My Uncle Bill Bailey had a mare named Flory who had been the leader of a wild herd. (Once in awhile, a mare led, but usually it was a stallion). Flory had been creased well down toward her shoulders and bore a considerable hole-scar in her mane where the bullet had struck. She must have been a good wild horse leader for, in her domesticated life, she took the lead. When we boys rode together on the prairies, she always insisted on leading the cavalcade of riders. And woe to the horse that tried to pass her!

Another method of horse hunting sometimes practiced on the plains was 'stalking'. In this, two or more men would select a certain bunch

Chapter 20: Wild Horses and Wilder Men

of horses and then, taking turn about, would ride or even walk on foot as near as possible to the herd. At the first approach of the stalker, the leader would race away, his drove of mares and colts following in great fright. But the oft repeated approach of the hunter brought a certain contempt for his presence. Soon the herd would only move when he came much nearer.

Now although a horse must sleep, he need not lie down to do so. He can sleep on his feet. Hence, the herd must be kept moving constantly with no time for sleep. Forty eight hours, at most, and the hunter could walk up to the sleeping herd and place a rope on aa many as he care to.

We boys used to also do this with wild birds. Selecting some one of the numerous birds, we would take turns running it about over the prairies forcing it to stay in the air as much as possible. After two or three hours of continuous flight, a fresh boy could easily run up and catch the exhausted bird.

Young rabbits, too, were caught in the same manner. Even old jacks sometimes died from overexertion when run into a hole in the sod by the shepherd dogs we used for cattle.

Old Eli Wolf, who lived up the creek from Bazine, had several good looking girls and several boys. Cap, his oldest, was a wild-horse man, and three of his girls were married to wild-horse men... Bill Keuffer, Saint Rowe and Charley Porter.

One day these three men brought a herd of wild horses to our place, selling my father and several of my uncles a pair of sorrels. It seemed this particular herd had been exceptionally fleet of foot and Keuffer was sure there was running blood among them.

The Wolf boys, Boot and Josh, also bought a choice sorrel from this bunch.

Father called the sorrel stallion he bought, Dick. The Wolf boys

Chapter 20: Wild Horses and Wilder Men

called theirs, Steamboat. Well, Dick and Steamboat became honest-to-goodness race horses, and were raced all over the Golden Range country from Nebraska clear down into the Pan Handle country of west Texas. Father, a great racehorse man, often bet his last dollar and even his coat on some race in which Dick was entered.

Steamboat was never quite the horse that Dick was. But he and Dick looked so much alike that, frequently, Steamboat would be matched for a race and Dick would run it.

The Wolf and Cole boys were great pals in those days as many a carnival outfit found out to their sorrow!

Wild-horse men were almost as wild as the horses they caught and tamed. They rode hard, lived hard, fought hard and, sometimes, died hard. In their quarrels, blood kin and in-law relationships were often forgotten for the moment.

One day, while in town, Saint Rowe and Wild Horse Bill had some sort of misunderstanding. Guns followed words, and the two brothers-in-law, would probably have killed one another had not the other brother-in-law, Cap Wolf, turned up. Cap, knowing better than to try and reason with them, laid a gun on either of them and made them drop their own.

"Now, git home, you two hot headed fools!" he ordered.

This they did. Bill to his own dugout some two miles south of town; Rowe to his place about the same distance north.

Cap took their guns along with him, later turning them over to their owners when they were in a better frame of mind.

Some of these prairie men had widely diversified talents. For instance, Charley Porter was a great stone cutter as well as a wild-horse man in those days. Many of the early day markers and monuments in the cemeteries of the area were his work. These stones he cut became not only

Chapter 20: Wild Horses and Wilder Men

a monument to the dead, but also to the memory of the man who fashioned them.

It was also Charley Porter who built the first wind mill that ever turned a wheel in the winds that blew across the Golden Range. As I recall, this old mill was made entirely of wood and was named, "The Eli", in honor of old man Wolf, Charley's father-in-law. It did service for many a year on the Porter homestead about two miles due north of town.

Last Charley also had considerable talent as a house builder. He helped his brother-in-law, Saint Rowe, build a stone house in the bank of a little draw that came out of the divide north and east of town. A house which held a strange fascination for me as a boy. How many times I have dreamed of being there once more, and of walking through its stony interior!

Possibly some of the very old settlers may remember it as it really was. But to me, it was a charmed house... haunted not by the ghosts of men and women but, rather, with the spirits of long departed ages. Made of soft, yellow stone, particular only to the banks of the draw where it was built, I have never seen its like in any other part of the country. The fact that Charley used this same stone for his tombstones as well may have caused me to associate it with forgotten things.

Not only had the architect finished the house inside as well as out with this yellow stone, but he had built in all manner of cupboards and tables and even the floor of the same soft yellow stone.

I used to think the place had been built by some ancient monk, even before the Flood of Noah's time... and that, if one was fortunate, he might somehow step back into that time.

The door was in the west (west doors have always intrigued me), as were the only two windows of the house. The rest of the walls were laid

Chapter 20: Wild Horses and Wilder Men

against the back of the draw. When the afternoon sun fell across the stone floor and lighted up the massive furniture and the little stone cubby holes and closets, one could just naturally imagine anything one wished.

Possibly it was this imagining that has been responsible for the thousands of dreams I have had throughout my life concerning this old house. Yet always it seems good to go back there, if only in dreams, and meet again the spirits that haunted the place for me.

Long after it had fallen in ruins, I herded my cattle around the old house and must confess it still intrigued me. Hawthorn had nothing on me. I had my Old Manse too. And I am certain it was just as mossy as his may have been... even if mine was only a wild-horse man's dugout in the bank of a draw.

21. Uncle Oll

Uncle Oliver Boarst was typical of many of the men who came to the prairies in those early days to carve a home from the wilderness. Not that he seemed much concerned with that home once it was carved... leaving, as he did, a great deal of the upkeep to my Aunt Clee and the seven children who came through the years.

The prairies in those days seemed to gender a roving spirit in the men who fought to tame them and Uncle Oll, as we called him, was no exception. For that reason, were I asked who was most responsible for conquering the west, I would say it was most certainly the women.

Some old timer has said that it was a good country for men and dogs, but hell on women and horses. Perhaps he was right. However, most of my acquaintances of those early years who are still living are women... the men having long since gone on.

The first generation of Coles, as well as the sons-in-law and daughters-in-law, are a dramatic example. Only the women remain. My mother at one hundred and two and Effie Lee who lived to be eighty-two. Also Aunt Belle, Jim's wife, and Aunt Nancy, Gill's wife... as well as several of the old neighbors. All women.

Being an idealist, I like to think that it was not the hardships that took the men so early but, rather, the restlessness engendered by the new lands. Those men were pioneers; pioneering was their calling. When, finally, there were no new lands to be conquered they just hitched up, as it were, and drove over the divide into newer country. Somewhere, off yonder beyond the horizon, they are waiting now for their women and children to come and help them with the celestial harvest.

Uncle Oll as has been stated, was one of those men. A man of many parts and many faces as the Coles discovered shortly after meeting him for

Chapter 21: Uncle Oll

the first time.

Father and Mother and Aunt Clee had gone down into eastern Kansas to look for work. A late spring snow storm forced them to spend one night at the hotel of the town where they happened to find themselves.

Aunt Clee, a rather striking type of girl, immediately attracted considerable attention. Scarcely had they registered when Oliver Boarst made his appearance. Introducing himself as the owner of the hotel, he begged the pleasure of Aunt Clee's company for the evening.

His was a whirlwind courtship. Before the evening was over, the two were engaged.

Father was not at all pleased, but my aunt had a will of her own. In less than a week, she and Oliver Boarst were married.

The very next morning after the wedding, she was asked to help in the hotel kitchen to pay for the room they had slept in. It seemed that Oliver Boarst, rather than being the owner of the hotel, was merely a hired chore boy! When cornered by the enraged Clee, he protested that, although this was, unfortunately, true, it had been his sincere intention to advance to the higher position... with his wife's cooperation!

After Clee's display of Cole temper, coming too late to do any good, they had no choice but to return to my father's camp and take up lodging there.

Uncle Oll was French and declared that fact in numerous ways. Grandpap Cole always shook his head when the French were mentioned, but he never said anything to Clee about Oll. Apparently, he seemed to think as much of Oll as any of his other sons-in-law.

We nephews and nieces thought him a fine fellow... especially since we were always welcome at his house, no matter how many might come nor how long they might stay.

Chapter 21: Uncle Oll

Aunt Clee was a great favorite with us as well. To us, her supply of plays, dances and the like seemed inexhaustible.

Sometimes when Uncle Oll was absent on one of his numerous trips about the country, rations got pretty low at the Boarst house. But he usually turned up in time to prevent a catastrophe... always bringing with him a great supply of provisions. Naturally, we thought we were lucky indeed to be visiting the Boarsts when Uncle Oll returned!

Some of the neighbors wondered just how Oll managed to get so much together in such a short time. Once or twice, officers of an eastern county were stricken with the same speculation. Uncle Oll did his time and succeeded in returning to the homestead without the family suffering too much. Once or twice, I think Grandpap donated a little, but most of the time Oll was equal to the occasion.

Although he and Aunt Clee spent two or three years in Colorado, burying a baby in Aspen during that period, they came back to the Golden Range just as Grandpap predicted they would.

Uncle Oll had a way with horses equal to that of any gypsy who ever camped beside the road. While Aunt Clee stayed at home and managed to keep feed for the stock in winter... and the mares and cows dropping their foals in season... Oll proceeded about his horse business.

The Golden Range was free in those days. A man who owned cattle or horses had only to turn them out on the grass and watch them increase. In this respect, the Boarsts profited along with the rest.

Sometimes my father used to wonder just where and how Oll got so many fine horses with so little effort. But since Aunt Clee could pretty well account for every head of them... and men were not questioned too closely in those days... the Boarst remuda boasted some splendid mounts.

As a matter of fact, the finest horse I ever owned... and I have

Chapter 21: Uncle Oll

owned some good ones... came from the Boarst layout. He was named Durok. A fine, high headed sorrel that could outrun anything on the range. In addition, he was sensible and quiet along with it. There was no prouder boy in the country than when I got my saddle on Durok and rode across the miles with my friends.

Sometimes, we were wont to question just where Uncle Oll managed to secure almost everything which he brought to the homestead. Perhaps we did him an injustice. He was always a good worker, and if there was work to be had in the neighborhood, Oll always had a job. Nor did he ever, get into any trouble that we were ever really sure about.

One fall, my Uncle Jake and Uncle Ira went with Oll into Indian Territory and were gone quite awhile. Later, Jake said that several times he became worried about the numerous, unexplained articles that kept appearing around Oll's wagon. However, when questioned about the matter, Oll said simply that he had traded for them.

Once Jake said, they were flat broke and without a bite to eat. Halting that night near a good sized town, Oll told them to make camp while he rode in and looked the place over. Filling his pockets with some of his 'unexplained' articles, he disappeared. Shortly after sundown, he returned with several days supply of provisions. Among other things, he brought back a huge wooden bucket filled with old fashioned paper wrapped caramels...twenty whole pounds of them!

Being strictly honest, Jake became alarmed lest the law hold them in account for Jake's entire outlay. Immediately, he demanded where and how Oll had gotten the stuff.

Oll quickly put his mind at ease. "Just traded for 'em," he said. "Got the candy throwed in for boot. Thought we might want a little dessert to go along with the steak an' things."

Chapter 21: Uncle Oll

The next day, Oll got a job in town, and the trio remained there several days. During this time, Jake claimed Oll treated every kid in town to caramels, never making any attempt to hide the big wooden bucket.

Good, bad or indifferent, that was Uncle Oll for you.

Just when Oll went away for good, I do not remember. Nor am I certain if any of the family knows of the date of his death or his place of burial. He just drove off one day, as he was in the habit of doing and never returned. When it became evident that he was not coming back, Aunt Clee took on the burden of the family and went forward with it like many a prairie woman before her. She traded the homestead for a hotel in town, ironically enough. Later, she sold the hotel and went to Arkansas where she died and is buried.

22. Some Prairie Inventors

Pap Cole always contended the Golden Range was the fairest land on earth, not excepting the Shenandoah Valley in Virginia. Moreover, he firmly expected some of the Range's sons and daughters to take their place among the mighty of the world.

"Virginia may be the mother of Presidents,' he said, "but the Golden Range should and will produce greater men than mere presidents."

This conviction seems to have been wide spread throughout the country. One prairie mother, when asked if her firstborn was to become a great lawyer, retorted: "If that's the best he can do, I'll take him out an' shoot him!"

Walter P. Chrysler, a man destined to take his place among the great industrialists of the world, was born in the little town of Ellis, Kansas... over the divide to the north of the Cole ranch. Walter Chrysler, like thousands of other boys born on the Golden Range, took his first ride on the back of or behind some prairie bronco. Later, he hitched one hundred and eighty of them to four wheels and left the prairie dust so far behind it became only a memory. His first home, much better than the average for the time, was a railroad shack built along the tracks and furnished gratis to the workers for the company. The seventy-seven story Chrysler Building in New York was builded on the foundation of that modest prairie home.

It pleases me to think that the grandeur and magnitude of the Golden Range country had much to do with these later accomplishments of Walter Chrysler's. Like the two lines of a triangle, the divergence may be small at the beginning, but, extended across a lifetime, who can say the length of the hypotenuse. The boy, the home, the beginning... so small and insignificant at first, but magnified by the mirages of that favored

Chapter 22: Some Prairie Inventors

land...how potent the afterglow! Nations have trembled and will continue to tremble because such men had their day. In a land such as ours, every mother's son has a chance to become president, but only the favored of the Gods may know the divine persuasiveness of lands such as the Golden Range.

"Some are born great, some acquire greatness, while others have greatness thrust upon them."

The Golden Range had nothing to offer the inquisitive but greatness, symbolized by the expansive miles reaching out from a common center in all directions. One either accepted this, or sank back forever into the nothingness from which he sprang. The prairie grass did not long retain the wheel marks of the transient, but the deep ruts of the old trail still declare the reality of the men who brought, produced and carried away.

George Washington Carver was the first Negro we had ever seen, and we were quite small when he first came into our lives... a tall, serious looking boy, who was to become one of the famous scientists of our country.

His homestead was about twenty-five miles up the creek from our old ranch and several miles from the first dugout and soddy. In those days, none of us had any idea that we were looking at one of the great men of the age. Like Lincoln, his greatness still slept within him.

Actually, he may not have been as tall as he seemed to us children. For since he usually came to town standing up in his ramshackle old wagon, this no doubt tended to make him appear taller than he really was. Just barely can I remember the team of ponies he drove hitched to that old wagon. To us children, they were 'ni***r' ponies because they belonged to a 'ni***r', and for that reason they were just a mite different from the thousands of other ponies we were familiar with. They were, I believe, a

Chapter 22: Some Prairie Inventors

bay and a very light sorrel... with just a little white in their faces. They were always very thin, very hungry and very thirsty. That a pleasant memory, therefore, to recall how he was always rubbing them down and talking to them as he gave them the rice corn or cane fodder he had brought all the way from his homestead on the upper reaches of the Walnut. "Way out by Beeler," we usually told one another.

Carver was a friendly fellow who generally had some word with my father or Pap when they met in the old wagon yard back of Phoebe Daniel's lumber yard. We lived about the same distance east of Ness City, the county seat, as George lived west. Quite frequently we would meet him in the wagon yard at feeding time. It was always a high light in the day's adventure to get to see the colored man. Ni***r or 'darky' we most always called him, my folks being from the South. 'Darky' was, strictly speaking, Missourian and Mother always used this term. 'Ni***r' was from farther South, and my aunt, Effie Lee, sure could make it plenty black when she used the word. However, I very much doubt if George Washington Carver ever had time to worry much about what white folks called him. He had his wagon hitched to a star and was busy getting those western ponies on out of the way... so that he might reach the divine heights his soul could see across the miles of Golden Range surrounding his homestead. He achieved his goal. His homestead has become a shrine for the humble of all races who struggle upward in the night toward dream-fulfillment.

Pap Cole was of the opinion that Joe Kiner could make anything he chose to if he had plenty of barbed wire.

"Give Joe a pile of green rails and a bale of wire," he vowed, "an' he'll make you a threshing machine, engine an' all!"

Sometimes, I think Pap was not far wrong, either. Especially when considering the numerous tales handed down from those days about the

Chapter 22: Some Prairie Inventors

mighty prowess of the little Iowa farmer who lived just across the creek from the Cole ranch.

Machinery of any kind was scarce on the Golden Range, and a good deal of that was crude and homemade. Nonetheless, Joe was always equal to the occasion. When the necessity arose he simply made what he wanted and went on about his work.

A classic example of Joe's ingenuity was a corn planter, made from Lizzie's only washpan. Wired in close behind the moleboard of his plow, one had only to fill the contraption with seed at the beginning of each round. Then when the furrow was complete, the corn was planted and covered; it needed, only the spring rains to bring it up. Other farmers, not so ingenious, had to plow and harrow first, then laboriously chop in the kernels with spade, axe or dibble. Joe's rows were always as straight as the plowed furrow; not so the average field.

There was one small drawback. Having only the single washpan, one of the children had to pour the water before meal time. But this was a small matter compared to the corn planting. Woman-like, though, Lizzy, Joe's wife, was always complaining while the pan was in use in the field... or when my father borrowed it for his planting after Joe had finished with his. (At the time, we had no washpan at our house, usually going to the nearby creek for our ablutions.)

But Joe was the best of neighbors, and Lizzy was only a woman and expecting again that spring... a condition which seemed chronic in most households of the Golden Range country!

There were eight Kiner children and eight of us little Coles with only the stream between us... and the shady banks of the creek a splendid place to pass away the hours of childhood. When asked why he had so many children, Joe always declared they were the only things he could get on time, without paying interest. There never seemed too many little

Chapter 22: Some Prairie Inventors

Kiners or Coles. The Golden Range was big and wide and the parents in both households were provident.

Despite Lizzy's constant complaining the washpan did service in both fields that springtime... and we boys still had time for play along the creek banks. Thanks to Joe Kiner's corn planter!

A couple of other examples of Joe's creative initiative. One spring day Joe struck a rock while planting corn, breaking the point, or nose off the plow. Any other man would have hauled it miles to the nearest blacksmith shop and wasted half a day waiting his turn for repairs. But Joe simply took a piece of wire and bound the point firmly in place until he finished plowing.

One summer, while making hay out on the divide, the sickle of the mowing machine picked up a bit of flint rock and was jerked in two before Joe could stop the team. In a short time, Joe had the thing wired together well enough to finish the afternoon's work. He was a genius with wire and never worried about anything as long as there was plenty of it handy.

Since the earliest settlements, there were always Timkins about. Over around Elsworth and Ellis and up at Hays. Down around Hoisington and, further east, over into Missouri. Quite a bunch of them. Nowadays, they have spread over into Texas and on out to Colorado.

To almost everyone, the name has a familiar ring to it. And when it is pronounced, one wonders where he has heard it recently. Open a current magazine to the machinery advertisements and there, in big lettering, you see it.

A fellow said to me just the other day, "Did you know the world runs on Timkin bearings?"

Naturally, I knew that. But I wonder if he could recall when there were no Timkin bearings. When the machinery of those days made such a

Chapter 22: Some Prairie Inventors

protest that young Hank Timkin couldn't sleep at night for thinking about it. The buckboards and wagons used in the buffalo hunts complained continually. The grindstone in the little blacksmith shop reminded him of the situation.

When he traveled west to the Golden Range country, the crude machinery of the day seemed always to be stridently complaining about a lack of grease. And, even when greased, often still squeaked and groaned. Hank looked out over the miles and miles of fertile land and wished in his German soul that he owned a big slice of that same land. He would show the world what a real wheat farm was like! Of course, the buffalo and the antelope would have to go first. And the farm machinery would have to be greatly improved.

Dreams! Dreams! Land cost money, and he had no money. Nothing but a persistent idea whirling around and around in his mind... until one day the idea crystalized. He made the thing down in the little blacksmith shop, and it worked. It's still working.

The buffalo and antelope are gone now, and virtually every kind of engine in the world runs on Timkin bearings. The farm on the Golden Range was bought with royalties, and a town, Timkin, Kansas, was named for the German boy who couldn't abide the squeak of a dry axle!

23. About the Knapps

My Aunt Lizzy seemed to have a weakness for Frenchmen. Or maybe they had a weakness for her. Anyway, my uncle, George de Void, had not been out of her life for long, before she met up with a young French-Canadian from the lake country of Minnesota named Eugene Knapp. Like his predecessor, he made quick work of capturing the 'young grass widow over at the Coles', as she was known.

Shortly thereafter, he came among us with the hearty good will of the entire family. I think even Grandma Cole was glad when the French-Canadian proposed taking Lizzy from the home roost. Although I always loved my aunts with a fidelity that sometimes surprised even myself, like my Uncle Jim once said about his sisters, I am sure glad I didn't have to marry any one of them.

Eugene Knapp was a splendid looking chap in his young days, one of the best looking men I ever saw. Light complexioned for a Frenchman, with brown hair and moustache, he had the build of a perfect man.

Gene, as we always called him... Uncle Jim called him Knappie... was a great wrestler in a time when the sport was but little short of murder. Although my father matched Gene for money against some of the greatest of that rough and tumble day, I never saw Gene conquered... only tied a few times. Several who met him in a bout never wrestled again. Somehow, when ever my uncle stripped for a tussle, I always thought of the perfect brute. He was that much of a man.

The only person ever to bring him under subjection was Aunt Lizzy... and that, only temporarily. Just so much would my uncle take from that source. Then he would hitch his ponies to the old wagon and depart for regions unknown. Sometimes, Lizzy would come home to Pap's, bringing the children along. Usually two or three days of that was enough

Chapter 23: About the Knapps

for all concerned. Gene would come back, Lizzy and the children would go home, the tension would lift at the Cole ranch and all would be lovely again.

In his time, Uncle Gene had been a great woodsman. He used to tell tall tales of the north woods which I doubted, but which I have since learned must have been every day life in those parts. He loved the big woods of Washington and Oregon, and spent much time there with his family in those early years. Yet always, they came home to the Golden Range. At last, they became owners of one of the largest horse ranches in the country.

Gene died there somewhere on the prairies. Just where he was buried, I never knew. However, I think it may have been at old Elkander in Scott County. In her old age, Lizzy went into Arkansas. She was buried at a place called King's Mills, or so I have been told.

Like my Uncle Oll Borst, Uncle Gene had raised another family before meeting Aunt Lizzy, but we of the Cole family never met any of them.

The Knapp-Cole marriage resulted in three children... Sylvia, Clyde and Edwin, in that order. As far as the Cole clan was concerned, Edwin was always the baby in more ways than one. But he became quite a man in the short fifteen or twenty years he lived on the Golden Range.

Clyde was a big, blustering, good natured sort of fellow given to much talking but little action. Still, he could always be depended upon in so far as his word was concerned.

Sylvia, a pretty, baby-like girl, was devoted to her brothers and the idol of her father.

We cousins of the Cole clan were always loyal to the Knapp group when they were absent, but, when they were present, we usually clubbed

Chapter 23: About the Knapps

together against them. The reason: self preservation. To put it bluntly, the Knapp boys were brutally selfish. The only way we could protect ourselves against them was to gang up. In like manner, the girls had to protect themselves against Sylvia and Aunt Lizzy. Uncle Gene never took much stock in our family brawls, generally letting us finish what we started. Not so Aunt Lizzy; she was always in the middle of things.

Against strangers, however, our whole attitude changed. Any of us would rather have had one of the Knapps for a sidekick than any other of the clan. Although I never saw Clyde in a fight, I once had to run a great bluff lest he and Edwin both take me to a cleaning.

Catching the two of them imposing upon some of the neighbor's children, I reported it to my Aunt Effie Lee. She, in turn, took it up with Aunt Lizzy. As usual, Aunt Lizzy would hear nothing against her children. And, naturally, I was a tattler of untruths.

Later, when the three of us were alone on the prairie, the Knapp boys decided it would be a good thing to 'thrash the hell out of me', as they put it, for even reporting the affair. Now either of them was bigger than me, (I was always small for my age), so I could see no way out of the scrape. Except to bluff. Taking a long chance, I squared my shoulders and dared them to make their try.

"But I'm warning you," I said with false confidence. "I can lick the daylights out of both of you with one hand tied behind my back."

The bluff worked.

"Well, I presume you could," Clyde said, and they got on their horses and rode away.

At a prairie picnic, Edwin got into an altercation with a boy somewhat larger than he.

"You big so an' so," he said. "You just ain't big enough to whip

Chapter 23: About the Knapps

me!"

Quite a level headed fellow, the other boy would much have preferred to let the matter drop, feeling, no doubt, that he was too much older and larger than Edwin. But nothing would satisfy my hot-headed cousin but a fight. So at it they went.

It really was some fight, too, lasting almost an hour.

Neither of the boys could seem to get the better of the other. But at last, the older boy's weight and size began to tell. After he finally got Edwin down and pummeled his face to jelly, he straightened for a moment and asked:

"You had enough?"

"No, you big son of a bitch!' Edwin whispered. "I tole you you wasn't big enough to whip me, an' you just ain't!"

After some more pummeling, the question was put again. Being unable to speak this time, Edwin could only shake his head. No!

The fellow got up and reached for his gun. "I guess I will just have to kill the damn fool. He ain't got sense enough to know when he's whipped."

The rest.af the boys took them apart and carried Edwin home, he being unable to walk.

In a race with his brother, Clyde, across the prairies, Edwin's pony stepped into a gopher hole and falling, killed the boy with a broken neck. Clyde later took the rest of the family into Arkansas and, I suppose, still lives there.

My cousin, Sylvia, really grew up into a pretty woman, as women went in those days of narrow waists and wide skirts. When she reached the advanced age of thirteen, my aunt threw open the Knapp door and said,

Chapter 23: About the Knapps

"Come on, boys!" and any number of prairie swains made a rush that way.

In those days, a girl usually settled such questions for herself, but I have heard several of my girl cousins declare that Aunt Lizzy never gave Sylvia a square deal with the boys... doing a great deal of the courting herself. Of course, then, as now, there may have been quite a bit of jealousy among the girls. I am not prepared to say. I do know that Sylvia, dressed for a prairie frolic, was a striking figure. It is safe to say she made many a prairie heart turn flip flops.

Once her brother, Clyde, and I hid in Sylvia's bedroom that we might gain first hand knowledge of how a girl was really put together. The waist line was what stumped us... that, and those great, wide spreading skirts with the bustle that stood out behind in such a provoking manner. Clyde was of the opinion that the bustle was a natural appendage, common only to girls, which could be raised at will, and to any determined height, by the girl herself. Much like we had seen the old rooster grouse raise the ruff around his neck when dancing about his hens on the booming grounds.

I felt much wiser about such things having, at one time seen something made of wires and covered with gauze hanging from a rafter in Cad Bunting's bachelor dugout. Moreover, I had heard him tell my Uncle Cass it was a bustle. Just how Cad said he came into possession of the thing has escaped me. I dimly remember him saying the school marm sure did paw around some when the darn thing came loose while he was dancing with her.

Anyway, I was willing to give Clyde's theory the benefit of the doubt, remembering how we had seen the men dehorn the wild cows of the range... and figuring that maybe Cad had got his bustle in some such manner.

Well, everything went off in a grand manner in the dressing room. Even yet, I can hear Aunt Lizzy telling Sylvia to hold her breath hard and

Chapter 23: About the Knapps

pull in her stomach while she, Lizzy, took up the slack of her corset with the lacing from behind. Finally, when no more could be gained in this fashion Aunt Lizzy had Sylvia lay across the bed while she, placing her knee in the small of Sylvia's back, secured the last quarter of an inch it was humanly possible to gain.

While Sylvia stood before the mirror thus reduced in waist line, Aunt Lizzy added petticoat after petticoat to the girl's wasp-like figure... and us wondering all the while how, in heaven's name, Sylvia could ever raise her bustle with all that weight of skirt pulling down around her!

Before the deal was over, I became convinced that Clyde had misjudged the human female, and experienced a great pride coming up within me at my superior, manly knowledge of such things. However, I was somewhat disappointed when the bustle was at last produced and snugly tied in place (where such things are worn), to find it only a home-made affair of rags and orange carpet chain.

Clyde let out such a grunt of disgust when he found out his mistake... disillusionment is always hard to take when it concerns the opposite sex... that Aunt Lizzy and Sylvia nulled us out from under the bed and sent us howling out to the barn where my uncle was readying the team to take the family to the dance.

Sylvia's love affairs finally simmered down to two of the prairie boys; a little Methodist preacher and a big Irish boy from over in 'North Ireland'. Bad blood had been between the two even before my cousin came between them. On different occasions, the Irishman had given the preacher several good drubbings through the years. The girl between them only made matters worse.

Finally, when the Irish boy sent word to his rival to stay away from his girl or 'else', the preacher got himself a six-shooter. One day in town, when the Irishman came upon him suddenly, the preacher killed him

Chapter 23: About the Knapps

outright in self-defense.

The preacher married Sylvia and they lived on the Golden Range for many years, raising a family of children. At last, they went with the rest of the Knapps into Arkansas where the little preacher died.

Calamity seemed always following my Aunt Lizzy!

24. The Beloved Physician

Memory is a heady wine pressed in the vats of Eternity by angel feet and doled out to the favored of the Gods in ever increasing portions. Youth smells the fragrance of the vineyard abloom on the hillsides and dimly discerns the possibility of the ripened grape. Mid-life would taste the fresh juice so soon flowing from the bruised fruitage. But to Age alone is the privilege of the seasoned vintage. Only the old may drink themselves drunk in ever increasing revels and be conscious of no remorse.

I remember! I remember! Or, When I was young! Or, again: In that day!

These may be used only by those who have counted the mile posts of a full life and who, Janus-like, may look in both directions at once.

He came into my life, this Apollo of the Old West, when I was still a very small boy. Today, as then, he still holds the high place in my admiration which I granted him.

The 'Beloved Physician' was not a physician at all, but, rather, the victim of a mistaken identity, My mother had been teaching me some lessons from the Bible and I had been very much impressed by the title, The Beloved Physician, granted to Luke, the writer of the third book of the New Testament. Therefore, when the tall, angular, rather rawboned young man climbed down off the big freight wagon up there in my father's quarry, south of town, I felt a great reverence for him... thinking he must be the Beloved Physician, Luke, about whom my mother had been reading.

Unable at this early age, to rightly divide the time, I was prone to find my heroes however ancient, in the men of my day and with whom I might come in contact. Charley Coventry, from down the creek, I was certain was George Washington. Charley must have been somewhat

Chapter 24: The Beloved Physician

mystified when I asked him where his little hatchet was. Dan Terry was always associated in my mind with Hercules, possibly because of the twelve tasks set this hero... especially the cleaning of the stables.

In my childish mind, Men became Gods and Women, Goddesses, and I found Nymphs and Satyrs in every vale, and the plum thickets and willow wastes were redolent of divine life. Surely, the Golden Range was a wonder world to me in that old time, and her people invested with the heroic!

Some have called me pagan because of this but "He called them Gods to whom the word of God came."...and most of my men and women were God fearing (I know I was) and felt no sacrilege in attributing divinity to the heroic characters of my childish acquaintance. Age and childhood are closely linked, and I feel myself today very much the pagan I was when still a small boy. Like Wordsworth, I might say:

"Great God, I'd rather be

a pagan, suckled in a creed outworn

so might I, standing on this Pleasant lea,

have glimpses that would make me less forlorn;

have sigh l of Proteus rising from the sea

and hear old Triton blow his wreathed horn."

My father was very much at home in the presence of the tall, young man, Luke, and appeared to feel no reluctance in making him a price on a load of stone posts he had come seeking. Often, I wished my prosaic father would be more Jupiter-like in his dealings with the heroes of my fancy. But the Beloved Physician purchased the load of stone posts and hurried away much as other men did, leaving me to wonder, in my childish fashion, just when he had found time to write his portion of the New

Chapter 24: The Beloved Physician

Testament.

Since then, I have learned my 'Beloved Physician' lived, even more than he wrote, his portion of the Divine Word... and still lives it. Quite a prolific writer about things pertaining to the Golden Range country, Luke will long be remembered for his writing as well as for the neighborly life he has lived among the Prairie people.

An old Indian scout, he saw considerable service in the Indian Wars of the West, but with a modesty peculiar to himself, he never had much to say about those things. Mostly he spoke and wrote about the prairies and the beautiful things he saw and felt as he went about the joy and wonder of living.

He had no use for the Indian, having suffered some terrible calamity at their hands. Much like Joshua of old, he felt himself called to clear the land of the Amelekite. He had a hand in the Dobe Walls fight, if I am not mistaken, and several others of the time. He rode the range and the long trail up from Texas. He has felt the sting of the bitter blizzard and the heat of the desert sun. But always, he has listened for the Still Small Voice that came after these things.

There is no apology for Beauty; she is justified of her children, and Luke always saw the beautiful. In the reach of far places, in the close up of the home field, in the starry meadows of heaven... always he saw that which was beautiful, and reflected it in his life and manner of living. The wind in the bunch grass played a symphony for his hearing, and the stars at night a melody of old song. Childhood and old age were colors on his palette, and, by mixing them with love, he brought forth a marvelous picture. The seasons were four strings on his lute, the weather changes the frets he fingered while playing his song of ages. His cattle listened; the horse he rode gave ear, and all his neighbors paused and said, "It is Luke singing."

Chapter 24: The Beloved Physician

In medieval times, the bards and minstrels were the recorders and recallers of historic events. On the Golden Range, when a dispute arose among us as to some occurrence of the past, it was Luke who settled the matter for us. And, generally, he made a note of it as well.

Now, most of the cowboys and range hands were good singers in those days. It was a part of their calling. The cattle had to be sung to on the bed grounds at night. I would not, however, leave the impression that Luke was a great vocalist. That would be a matter of opinion. But Luke's songs were heart songs, heard as well in the recanting of some common, everyday event as in the singing of a prairie ballad. Pan-like, he seemed, to me, the personification of Nature. And with Milton, I could sing: "Universal Pan, Knit with the Graces and the Hours in dance, Led on the eternal spring.

Guardian of our fields and farms, all the old land marks were known to him, and many a dispute over such matters was settled by his word. In later days, whenever we wished to know where the old trails had been and where they led, it was Luke calling upon his abundant memory, who led us unerringly to some ancient Landmark and, from thence, pointed the way the men of old had gone.

A young land could not have thrived without such as he, nor the old know peace save he gave council. How rich his memory! How generous his sympathy!

"Luke, why do they call this barren draw The Hackberry," I asked one day, "when there is never a tree of any kind in all its miles?"

"It was not always so, Ira," replied Luke. "Years ago, an old hunter and trapper named Berry, Heck Berry, lived here-abouts on its banks. In those days, we called it Heck Berry's creek. The years have wrought the change...from Heck Berry to Hackberry. And so it stands today."

Chapter 24: The Beloved Physician

Again: "The old trail went somewhere here," said the young surveyor, seeking a route for the new road that was to cross the creek. "But exactly where?"

"Ask Luke," said his older companion. 'He will know. There may be quicksand here. There was none at the old crossing."

Two miles above the spot, Luke showed them the ancient ruts of the old trail...and the solid bottom of the prairie creek.

"That's Pisgah there to the west," Luke said one day. "Twelve miles from here to there as the crow flies. In the old days, we spied out the country from its peak and the trail came down this side. Off to the south, if we be on its top, we could see Dodge when the mirage was right. And Larnard off east. Sometimes, Hays was even lifted into view. I tell you, boy, the prairie air was as clear then as the waters of a prairie stream.

"Even the buffalo had a hard time hiding from us. And from the top of that hill no Indian could long conceal his camp. Down the Walnut, twenty miles, the smoke of his signal fires was an open book to us trail men. And the soldiers at Zara used to wonder sometimes at our knowledge of their doings!"

The rogue, the outlaw, the thief had no use for men like Luke. But we common folk loved him dearly. Now, when most of that ilk have moved on over the divide and only a few of his companions remain, Luke is still loved and respected by all who know him. He is still the Beloved Physician. The young of today, like the young of his youth, pay him the respect of listening when he speaks. And still is he the scout and guide to all who journey down the trail of life through the land he calls his own -

The Golden Range.

25. The Scotts

There was no water to be had on the high divide between the Pawnee and Walnut creeks. A fact which old Alvah Scott discovered to his sorrow... after he had spent the sale price of his Iowa corn land putting up one of the finest stone houses ever built on the Golden Range.

Viewed from the north side of the creek, the divide seemed a most intriguing place, well above the miasmatic vapours of the intervening lowlands, and yet low enough to be considered bottom by one used to the fields of the prairie state Alvah had just turned his back upon. In effect, an ideal place for the two story stone house which was to be the consumation of old Alvah's dreams.

What Alvah, as well as countless others in those early years, could not see was the prehistoric formation of ancient land, builded atop the permanent flow of waters coming down from the glacial thaws far toward the Dakotas. Just why this ancient formation should have been superimposed above the glacial flow, I do not know. But there it is, and there it has been since the ancient waves of the cretaceous seas piled it, layer on layer, above the water bearing sands. The transient flow of later days, coming down from the high lands toward the west, had cut away all of the soft uppercrust and brought in a sand and water level far above the ancient flow... but confined only to the narrow channels of the eroded beds.

The creek bed, with its abundant seepage, seemed to promise an abundant supply of water. When old Alvah and his son Linas, looked out across the miles toward the divide, they made the same mistake as many others in assuming this seepage underlay all the prairies to the south... even as far as the Pawnee and other streams winding their way across the country in those directions.

Chapter 25: The Scotts

As soon as the new house was finished, the Scotts turned their attention to making a well. Up until this time, they had hauled water from the creek three miles to the north. Now, instead of water, they found only the dry folds of this ancient formation deep below the black soil of their prairie holdings.

Linas had homesteaded the quarter west of the stone house and here, it is true, he did find an intermittent flow of brakish alkali water that could be used for the stock whenever, the rains came for any period over the divide. But this water always disappeared long before the summer was over. Then the stock had to be driven the three or four miles to the creek at least once a day for a drink. But then homesteading always had its problems, most of which were resolved one way or the other.

Once it had been lifted to its position in the thin, clear air of the prairies, the stone house on the divide became a landmark of consequence in those early days. Newcomers from the east swelled with hope and pride when it came into view, each secretly vowing to build one just like it when they had their first crop. Across the miles travelers sighted the glistening walls and hastened forward, hoping to find food and shelter for the night. If the well on Linas' quarter was flowing, well and good. If not, the animals must wait until the creek was reached. The barrel as the stone house usually contained enough for the man, though, sometimes one must wait until it returned from its trip to the bottom.

On a clear day, the house could be seen for a distance of forty miles. Many a freighter from Larnard or Dodge guided himself across the miles by keeping it in his line of vision. Wild horse hunters knew it was there, and cowmen moved their herds across the prairies by its guiding presence, knowing the creek was only an hour's drive beyond and much nearer if they were going south. The first mail carriers from Larnard to Bonny Doon on the creek and the county seat on toward the west

Chapter 25: The Scotts

sometimes stopped over at the stone house and ate dinner. Or, if delayed, stayed the night.

For the most part, these carrier trips were routine and often tedious journeys. But, now and then, something happened on a trip to brighten the driver's life. On one such trip, the mail carried a passenger bound for the new country toward the west. A well heeled individual, having on his person a wallet containing several thousand dollars in currency.

The carrier had planned to make the Scott house for the night and Bonny Doon the next morning for breakfast. But at dust, with no water at the stone house for the horses, he was forced to drive on in the dark and ford the creek to the post office at Bonny Boon.

Before leaving Alvah's place, word somehow reached the driver that road agents were following the outfit, expecting to rob the stranger with the money. Therefore at Bonny Doon, while old man Forbes and his boys helped take care of the mail and the mail carrier's horses, the stranger slipped away in the dark and over the bank into the draw that comes down to the creek there. Slipping his wallet under the roots of an old elm tree that still stands there, he make his way back to the house without having been missed by the driver or the Forbes men.

That night the mail sack was plundered, as well as the mail man and the stranger. However, a trip to the old elm the next morning found the wallet and its contents safe. Shortly afterward, the stage went on its way much as it had come the night before. To the stranger, looking back across the miles to the stone house it seemed to be a good place to be away from. For there had been no single tree there to hide so small a thing as a wallet.

To me, the old stone house on the divide seemed such a romantic place. As a little lad, I can remember building mighty castles in the air with nothing more substantial than its stony walls and the shimmering

Chapter 25: The Scotts

mirages that seemed always to lift it above the common earth of the surrounding prairies.

Here, it seemed, if one only had the ability, might be discovered all the phantom creatures Ever dreamed about. I knew there were prairie nymphs in the sunflower forests along the divide. And, sometimes, when the sun was right a bunch of satyrs would come over the cloud mountains to the west and hold revel around the old walls. Pegasus was wont to rest in the shade along the eastern front, and early mornings almost aways found fairy folk dancing in the dew of the short grass, or among the crocus blossoms that sprung up about the western door.

But noon was the saddest, sweetest hour of the day. Often at that time, I left my pony grazing in the yard or sleeping in the shadow of the northern wall while, awed and frightened, I slipped through the haunted portals of the western door and, climbing the rickety old stairs, looked out over the miles and miles or prairie, as far as the eyes could reach. Looked and dreamed such dreams of grandeur and glory and wonder no pen could ever record.

Long after old Alvah and Linas and the girls had moved on, I often brought my cattle up over the divide and fed them on the abandoned fields and pastures that seemed so wonderful to the Scotts in the-days that were gone. Then while the cattle were feeding, the old house became my castle. As lord of the manor, I gathered my retainers about me and held high revel.

Sometimes, I became so full of my day dreaming and the great events that transpired there about the old house that my sleep at night would betray me.

"Poor little kiddie," my grandmother would shake her head and murmur. "The sun must have teched him a mite yesterday!"

Years afterward, men hauled the stones of the old house away and

Chapter 25: The Scotts

now only the memory remains.

26. Old Fort Zimmerman

In reviewing the years since the first settlement was recorded on the Golden Range, I am continually impressed by the fact that someone always seemed to be just a little bit earlier than the last fellow recorded. And, of course, that surprise was reflected in those who were not quite as early as they thought.

Old Alvah Scott, coming over the hill from the north and driving down onto the Walnut bottoms, drew up sharply at sight of the long, stone house standing back a few rods from the creek bank. Feeling himself to be first settler in that part of the country, he was naturally surprised to discover that others had preceded him. Moreover, from the size of the place and its surroundings they had been here for some time.

He sat a moment, silently inspecting the house. With its great, deep earthen roof, iron barred windows and even a well and bucket with pulley almost in the doorway, this was clearly no ordinary house.

Nor, he discovered a moment later, was the man who inhabited it an ordinary individual. But then old man Zimmerman never claimed to be a run of the mill type. Uncouth in speech and appearance, he came charging around the corner of the house, swearing with every step.

"What the hell is all this?" he yelled. "Who are you?

Where did you come from? And what the ungodly hell do you want?"

Even profanity has changed with the years. Many of the current phrases of that day would be quite unintelligible now. But old man Zimmerman was a past master at the art of plain, fancy and embroidered 'cussin'. It was said he could combine more picturesque language in a single sentence than any man who ever lived on the prairies.

Chapter 26: Old Fort Zimmerman

Now, facing the newcomers, he seemed determined to protect that reputation.

Alvah Scott, like his son, Limas, who carried on after him, was a quiet man, not given to an excess of words. Therefore, masking his surprise and resentment, he waited for the flow of sulfurous language to cease. Practical considerations also entered into the matter. For the Scott caravan of loaded ox wagons had to find a crossing over the creek before it could reach the divide, dimly discernable in the hazy distance. This loud-mouthed old man might be able to help them.

He could... and did.

"By all the powers in Hell, Heaven and the Hereafter," old Zimmerman swore. "they should be put across the creek! An' that in damn short order, too!"

Producing an extra yoke of steers, he led the caravan some distance up the creek where he snatched it across to a great flow of language and tobacco juice.

Afterward, Scott never seemed able to locate the exact spot where the old man guided them across the creek. However, he came to the conclusion that if men were judged for every idle word, that crossing must have been recorded both in heaven and the underworld as well!

Old man Zimmerman was one of those legendary characters, common to the prairies, whose existence was disputed by some, believed in by others and allowed for by still others... but of whom no one seemed to be absolutely certain. The only thing about him that everyone seemed agreed upon was his excessive flow of vitriolic language. This attribute of character seems to have passed into history after having reached perfection in the person of the old man alone. For among all the thou-sands of professional linguists who had their day on the Golden Range, none was

Chapter 26: Old Fort Zimmerman

aver able to hold a candle to Zimmerman. He passed on across the Range, the personification of a big heart and a bigger mouth.

The old Zimmerman house still stands on the north bank of the creek. Even now, it is still associated in the minds of men with Indian times. As a boy, I remember it was called Zimmerman's Fort. That it was built for just such a purpose I am virtually certain.

Recently, proof has been produced that old man Zimmerman did not build the house himself, but came into possession of it through some of his kin who preceded him by several years on the Range. A family by the name of Abbott or Abblot seems to have been responsible for the building. At least they lived there before Zimmerman came swearing across the plains. Presumably, it was they who hauled the rock across the creek from the south ridge and fashioned the wall and dug the old well in the very doorway. The country must have been heavily infested with Indians, for the house was so built that it would have been very difficult to take by storm. Especially with determined, well-armed defenders behind its walls.

Lime was being burned along the creek in kilns dug for this purpose as early as the Scott's arrival. Once I found the ruins of an old blacksmith shop in the bank above one of these kilns where there was much old time iron... and a quantity of iron rods similar to those over the windows of the old fort. Where this iron came from, one can only guess, as well as who had the ambition and foresight to haul it the hundreds of miles from the foundry across the wilderness to this beginning of civilization. Only God, Himself, could tell the little things like this that conquered the wild places of the earth, for they were never recorded.

The walls of the fort were built of surface rock picked up from along the ridges across the creek (there is no rock of any kind on the north side), and put together with clay or a native lime probably coming from

Chapter 26: Old Fort Zimmerman

the same rocky ledges. Despite the passing years, the walls are still in perfect condition... even though I doubt if any repair work has been done in the past fifty years.

My first brother was born in this old fort some sixty five years ago and with the exception of a new shingle roof, it looks much as it did then. There is little evidence of tool work on the stones that comprise the walls. What little does appear seems to be that of a smooth edged chisel. The original roof was of ridgepole and rafter, with a great depth of native lime covering all. No Indian arrow could ever have set fire to it. Nor were the rains so plentiful then as to wash it thin. To my knowledge, the roof never leaked. But then it would have taken a long rainy spell to have soaked through the almost three feet of magnesia soil that comprised that roof.

Since the days of the Scotts and the crossing of the creek under the direction of old Zimmerman, there has always been a plowed field between the fort and the creek. On that day, potatoes were growing in the field, as well as corn and a few striped watermelons.

What an aggravation this field was when, in later years, I had to keep constant watch over my herds when they came to the creek for water! Had they pillaged the field, I would have been held responsible for whatever damage was done. And, as any old-timer knows, cows can do plenty of damage!

But then that was a part of everyday life on the Golden Range, and made that life no less wonderful!

27. The Passing Show

The Coles did not remain long on the homesteads in the big swale. As soon as they were able to give deeds to the land, they sold out to a fellow by the name of Dively and moved on up the creek nearer the new town of Bazine.

This Dively had quite a bit of money for the times, and a great desire to found a big cattle ranch in this new west.

"We might just as well let Dively have these places," Pap Cole said. "He's already bought up every, thing around us. If we stay, we won't be able to run any sizeable herds... like we'd planned. Besides, we can get those Long claims up there above Bazine for considerably less than Dively's offering for these. Also, if we move fast, there's a chance of getting a preemption and possibly a tree claim up that way."

Soberly, they thought it over. The railroad had come, even as young John had predicted, following the line of least resistance along the section line that formed the north boundary of the Cole land. Now-a railroad fence five wires high heralded the end of the old days of freedom.

So they sold out and bought the Johnny Long claims on the south side of the creek just across from old Fort Zimmerman. Purchasing cattle with some of their homestead money, they soon became cattlemen in their own right...with an almost unlimited range stretching away toward the south and over the divide.

Grandad Cole moved his family into a two room stone dugout in the east bank of the creek that had belonged to one of the Longs and, of course, went with the land. My father and mother moved into a one room stone dugout a little way up the creek. It was here that memory first began in my life. And, even now, the little stone house seems the most wonderful place in the world.

Chapter 27: The Passing Show

The men of the family took up tree claims adjoining the newly purchased land. In the following years, they were kept busy getting the old ranch shaped up for the cattle industry that was to follow. Grandma Cole was never quite satisfied with these 'up the creek' claims, always contending that the Coles would have done much better had they retained the homesteads and become farmers instead of cattlemen.

There was a period in the settlement of the Golden Range country known to all the old settlers as 'The Boom'. Its duration is as sharply etched in the history of the west and in the memory of the old timers as any of the wars that have marked the building of the country.

The prediction, made by Pap Cole, of a family on every quarter section was certainly fulfilled in the two or three years of this incredible era. Only God knows where they came from, these settlers who fought and struggled and quarreled over the land, and then, in bitter disappointment, went away again into nowhere... leaving only a mound of earth where a soddy had been, or a hole in the bank of a draw to mark the location of a dugout. Only God could remember the hope and high endeavor, the dismay and remorse, the chagrin and despair of those years. They came, they fought to gain the land, they fought to retain it...and, in so short a time, they fought to free themselves from its powerful clutches.

"Stay until you get your feet wet an' you'll never leave," was a near-truth in the lives of those who came, and who went away as well.

The hope of the springtime was never quite fulfilled in the fruitage of the autumn. Hope on the Golden Range was a perennial growth that withered with the coming of autumn, but whose roots reached deep into the prairie soil and lived aver always to the coming of another Spring. Even the prairie flowers declared this truth, the greater number of them being perennial and, living a great measure in the future, produced only when the favored years appeared. But, oh, what beauty, what a wealth of color and what fragrance when this came about!

The Passing Show

There was no grain for the team that spring. Nor would there be any in the autumn unless the prairie sod was broken and seed somehow gotten into the land. The horses, too weak to graze, were slowly starving to death. Sometimes the neighbors came and helped get them on their feet so that they could gather a few bites of the greening prairie grass. Meanwhile, Henry grimly pounded out the lay of the rod plow, readying it for the few rounds the horses might manage.

Silently, the woman moved about her chores, her body already big with child. Sometimes, she helped lift the horses, but her strength, too, was limited. She could only do so much.

Watching Henry chopping into the sod with the axe the seed for the fall crop, a great pity welled up within her. Pity for him... and a great despair for the two of them. So few furrows the horses were able to claim before they were loosed to gain strength for another day!

Worse, like her and the horses, Henry was growing weaker by the day. Ricecorn flapjacks and sugar syrup were not enough to keep a working man going. Yet the man never said a word about being hungry. As a matter of fact, he never complained about anything much. He just... endured.

She wished she was strong like him. She wished she didn't keep thinking and dreaming about bacon and eggs all the time. No one would ever know just how she craved a single strip of bacon! Nor with what relish she ate the two or three prairie chicken eggs still fresh enough for food that Henry had found while plowing the day before. Of course, she knew it must be her condition. She would be much better when the baby came in June. Maybe the horses would be stronger, too. And the crop

Chapter 27: The Passing Show

should be in by then. Perhaps they would be able to take the baby home to her mother's for a few days. Perhaps...

But, meanwhile, this everlasting lifting of the horses always left her with a pain in her side and a great dizziness in her head.

Henry was away at the north end of the field, coaxing the weary old horses to do another round, when the great darkness settled over her that morning. He knew nothing about it until near noon, when he came in for a drink of water and found her lying on the dirt floor of the soddy, near the north window.

That afternoon, they dug a little grave under the wild beet plant at the northwest corner of the house and buried the son that was to have gone home with them in June. Afterward, Henry walked three miles for a bucket of water so that she might have a fresh drink. In such ways did he show his love.

The wild beet plant was perennial and still lifts its feathery fronds above the little grave at the northwest corner of the mound that was once a house. Long ago, the short grass took over the field, and the bones of the old team are bleaching somewhere at the end of a furrow.

Only God knows the whereabouts of she and Henry. But where ever they are, their hearts are always in the short grass near the wild beet bush.

The prairies never forget. Nor they who have felt the hope of her Springtime.

****

Pap wanted to buy the old buffalo gun, but the grizzled scout was adamant in his refusal.

"Gave her away once, a long time ago," he said. "Thought she was

Chapter 27: The Passing Show

gone for good that time; but then I got her back. Now I aim to keep her. Ain't much use for them kind of guns anymore nohow. Them modern Winchesters with their reloading outfits, are really, a much handier gun. But old Liz there, an' them rim fire shells o' her'n, sure had their day, on the buffalo ranges. By God, Mr. Cole, I once killed an old bull usin' Liz there, shootin' a good quarter of a mile! Had to have a rest though; she's a heavy old bitch!"

"You said somethin' about givin' her away once," Pap said, sensing a story. "Mind tellin' me why?"

"Well, it was on this wise." Refilling his pipe, the old scout shifted his chair a little more in the shade.

"Ike Cooper an' me had been stalkin' horses out there on the head waters of White Woman Creek that summer. Only they didn't call it White Woman Creek then. Had some outlandish Cherokee name for it. Leola or Leota... meanin' prairie flower'. Never was very much on that Cherokee jibberish myself. Now you take the Sioux or the Cheyenne... never bothered me a bit. I could swing their lingo good as them.

"Anyway, as I was sayin', we had our camp here in the breaks, so's to be near water, an' were walkin' the horses on the flats to the south an' west.

"I was in camp that mornin'. Ike was out with the horses. 'long about ten o'clock, guessin' by the sun, the most dilapidated outfit I ever set eyes on comes staggerin' into camp. When he gits close enough, I see he's a Cherokee. Couldn't call him a 'brave'; just warn't nothin' brave about him. Knew he was a Cherokee by some tribal marks fresh painted on his hide. All he was wearin' under God's heaven was a gopher skin clout tied aroun' his belly with a piece of rawhide. Thing that got my ninny though was a Cheyenne cradle board with a whimperin' papoose tied in it... a hangin' from his shoulders!

Chapter 27: The Passing Show

"Before I c'n say 'How', or even spit, that buck swung the cradle board to the ground an' started pourin' water down the papoose's throat like nobody's business, the kid a helpin' all he could with the chore. Pretty soon the whimperin' let up. Then the buck proceeded to fill his own dirty hide out of the old buffler horn he'd used to water the kid.

"When he finished, I gave him a piece of roasted hump which he wolfed like the starved critter he was. But 'fore he ate a bite, he pointed to a piece of raw fat and then to the baby. I nodded an' handed him my knife. Sure would a done your heart good to a seen that little bunch o' copper tear into that buffalo fat!

"Well, after I made him understand I could take his Cheyenne...me not wantin' to smear my conscience with his Cherokee... I got this story out of him.

"He was a Cherokee, alright. Born way off somewhere south in the Cherokee country. But while he was still a little shaver, he was stolen by the Cheyennes and taken north... somewhere into Montana or Canada. Adopted by the Cheyennes... I never been able to understand why a Cheyenne would want to adopt a Cherokee... he grew up an' married into that tribe. His squaw died when Little Buck, as he called the kid, was born. For some reason, the Cheyenne women didn't want to have anything to do with the little 'half breed'. So when an epidemic of measles struck the tribe, this buck slipped away with his son, determined to find his own people far to the south.

"Feedin' the kid was a problem from the start. The buck had an old gun very similar to old Liz. An' as long as his ammunition lasted, he managed to kill a wet buffler cow a day, feedin' the baby the warm milk. Two days before, his last shell spent, he threw the gun away, along with most of his camp gear. Travelin' light, he hoped to reach Cherokee country, or at least a bunch of Cherokee hunters.

Chapter 27: The Passing Show

"But luck was agin' him all the way. If he hadn't stumbled on my camp, I doubt if both of 'em would ever a got through. As t'was, the kid had had only three kildee eggs in two days; the buck nothin.

"Well, I couldn't keep the beggar. Had no use for a darn Cherokee nohow. The best I c'd do was give him old Liz and what ammunition I had an' kick him out o' camp. Ike 'lowed I was the biggest fool he ever met. Offered to bet me ten to one I'd never see my gun agin. I wouldn't bet.

"Three years later, over south of Dodge, I woke up one mornin' with old Liz a lyin' by my side. Damndest thing. You think you got one o' them varmints all figgered out... an' then he does somethin' like that. Makes you mad as hell 'cause he's double crossed you. He ain't done what he was supposed to do. Yep, makes you mad... an' a mite ashamed. Keep tellin' myself ain't no good Injun but a dead 'un. But ever since then, it's been kinda hard to believe.

"No, Mr. Cole..." The old scout knocked the dottle from his pipe and smiled quietly at Pap. "I just reckon I'll keep old Liz to help me remember that Injun. Bet there ain't another one like him in the whole damn west!'

Pap said nothing. The two of them sat there, staring out across the gently rolling prairie, each immersed in his own thoughts, as dusk crept quietly over the land.

****

After starving on the prairies for some time, Tom Smith finally decided he'd had enough. Loading up what goods he could, he drove back to his wife's folks. Behind him he left a perfectly good dugout, with a fine 'car' roof of 1' x 12' pine boards and 2' x 12' rafters. For several weeks the dugout sat there unmolested on the prairies. Until my father and several of his neighbors... each without the others knowledge... decided that it would

Chapter 27: The Passing Show

be a shame to let the dugout roof rot out there on the prairie.

On a certain moonlight night, (perhaps it was a moonlight night that gendered the idea to begin with), Cap Wolfe drove alongside the dugout and proceeded to remove the sod and dirt covering from the roof planks. This done, he was just in the act of filching the first of the planks when he heard the squeaking axle of an approaching wagon. Cap swore softly. It would never do to be caught swiping a neighbor's roof in the middle of the night. Hurriedly, he drove his team and wagon down over the bank of the draw and waited for the approaching wagon to go by. To his chagrin, instead of passing on, the wagon turned in alongside the dugout which he, Cap, had so recently fled! A moment later, Bill Keuffer, one of Cap's numerous brothers-in-law, jumped down from the wagon and looked the situation over.

Deciding that luck was with him, he proceeded to remove the planking from the roof... while Cap ground his teeth in helpless frustration. Having stacked the planking in a nice even pile, Bill then turned his attention to the three or four 2' x 12's. Loaded first on the running gears of the wagon they would make a good foundation for the shorter timber. He had just accomplished this when the sound of an approaching wagon froze him in his tracks. Feeling, as Cap had done before him, that it would never do to get caught, he hurried his team down over the bank of the draw. There, somewhat farther down than Cap's hiding place, he waited for the stranger to pass on. To his consternation, he saw my father's team pull up alongside the neatly stacked pile of lumber!

Deciding it was his lucky night, Father loaded up the conveniently stacked lumber... while Cap and Bill Keuffer gnashed their teeth in the shadows. The job completed, Father climbed back in his wagon and drove home. His unsuccessful, disgruntled 'competitors' followed in their own good time. It was several years later before the story was finally pieced

Chapter 27: The Passing Show

together. After that, Cap and Bill always referred to my Dad as "Slicker John."

****

On the Golden Range, in those early years, necessity was quite frequently the handmaid of thrift, or vice versa, as the case might be.

"Necessity compelled us to stay," my father used to say. "We just didn't have anything to get away on, even had we been inclined to go."

Those who left generally gave what few possessions they could not take along, to their friends. Some, less considerate, simply drove away and left what they could not take with them. Whoever found it first, appropriated it. But woe to him if he was caught in the act! His neighbors although like minded, could and would and did always point the finger of scorn at him. If they dared.

One example, more amusing than serious, involved the 'partial appropriation' of some wooden fence posts.

Joe, a very thrifty soul who lived along the creek, owned a quarter section of land farther out on the prairie. This quarter he fenced with wooden posts cut along the creek. Being of a frugal mind, he decided that a seven foot post would be more economical than a five foot one. In a few years, he reasoned, the post would rot off in the ground and would have to be replaced. But with the seven foot pole, he would have only to lower it into a mew hole... the exposed part being well seasoned by the prairie air. Despite the fact that the fence was somewhat top-heavy and subject to considerable ridicule from his neighbors, he was well pleased with his new fence.

Now Bill, another frugal soul pressed considerably by necessity, lived some ten miles or so beyond the divide. His land was treeless and, for fuel, he was compelled to pick up cow chips over the prairies. No one

Chapter 27: The Passing Show

liked to pick up cow chips; it was an onerous job. Bill was no exception. Passing by the new fence on his way home from town one day, his mind recoiled at the inexcusable waste of good wood in the top heavy affair. Something, he mused, ought to be done about it. And he was the man to do it. Coming back the following night with his wife for a driver, he bucksawed the tops off the overlong posts. The result: a fine load of good wood come the cold days of winter.

Joe never missed the tops of his posts until the next spring when he went over that way to do some plowing.

Sometimes Bill's neighbors twittingly called him Bill 'Topper!'

28. Curley

"Why don't you get rid of them warts, kid? Kids around these parts sure make me think of south Texas cattle... all bumped up with warts and wens and ringworms like they might have been drinkin' brack water out of the resackas. Just no excuse runnin' around in that condition at all! What are you all anyway? Some kind of dogie stock?"

It was 'Curley' speaking. Curley Hatcher, as we were wont to call him out of his immediate presence; Mister Hatcher when near enough for his piercing eyes to take account of us. 'Old Curley', sometimes, when none of the older folks were about. But always Mister Hatcher in his presence.

"Sure wish I could get rid of the doggone things," I said, conjuring up in my mind a drove of the scrawny south Texas stock such as were sometimes driven by my father's ranch. "Just might be I got the blamed things off 'n that steer Sote Kiner and me was tryin' to ride here a while back."

"A tryin' to ride! An' just why didn't you ride him? Never was the color of a longhorn's eyes I couldn't ride when I was your age! Anyway..." He pursed his lips thoughtfully. "I suppose you could get warts maybe from mangy stock. Ought to be a law against bringin' such stuff into the country. But if you want to really get rid of those warts, kid, I can take 'em off. An' it won't hurt a mite either."

I said I'd be much obliged if he would relieve me of the unpleasant squatters on my private property.

"Well, then, I'll take them off right now," Curley said, turning his piercing eyes on my bare feet and legs. "An' remember, kid... you better leave the toads alone after this.

Chapter 28: Curley

"You ain't foolin' me a bit, boy. I saw you an' that Kiner kid a ridin' that longhorn other day. I'd say wasn't either of you on him long enough to get warts... or anything else! An' one thing I do know...ain't nothin' like toad piss for makin' warts!"

With that remark, Curley rode away.

That night, it rained hard, and for the next couple of days, Sote Kiner and me were kept pretty busy trying out the numerous swimming holes scattered about over the range. Always in the summer, if it was a wet season, we prairie boys spent the greater part of our time in the water.

A few days later, after the water holes had dried up somewhat, I again met Mister Hatcher. Riding up alongside my horse, he said without preamble:

"What happened to your warts, kid?"

Looking down at my bare legs and feet, I was amazed to discover the warts were entirely gone. Bewildered, I could only stammer, "Gosh, Mister Hatcher, I don't know!"

"Well, I know," Curley said. "I told you I could take them off... an' I did. But mind you now...leave them blamed toads alone, or else something worse than warts will be gettin' holt of you!"

After Curley had gone, I got down off my horse and had a good look all over my body. There wasn't a single wart to be found! Only some pale white spots where the larger of them had been. From that day to this, I have never had another wart.

My Uncle Gil found Curley one summer when he went down into New Mexico looking for work. Gil was a wonderful horseman and Curley had a big horse ranch down in that country. Endee was Curley's headquarters and post office; he also had a considerable trading post there. There may or may not have been a railroad into Endee then; possibly, there

Chapter 28: Curley

isn't even any now. At any rate, a great part of my uncle's work was freighting to and from Curley's store. Although Curley bought wool and hides and did a general merchandise business, horses and mules were his main interest... along, probably, with cattle.

Sometime that summer, Curley got into trouble with one of the Mann boys who had ranches in those parts. Being pretty quick on the draw, Curley rode away from the place. The neighbors hauled Mann away in a buckboard.

Sensibly, Curley decided to seek a healthier climate. When my uncle gave him directions to the ranch on the Walnut, the horse rancher wasted no time in riding there.

Later that summer, Gil helped settle up the business at Endee. Then, bringing out a bunch of Curley's horses, he, too, came home.

For almost six years, Curley lived there with us on the Walnut. At last, when all the stock from Endee had been siphoned into Kansas, he bought himself a barber shop at Ness City and went into business again. He left our country sometime before World War I. For a long time, I never knew just where he had gone. But not long ago, while reading Frank Dobie's book, The Mustang, I found him again at Myrtle Point, Oregon. He was still telling his tales when Dobie found him, as attests The Mustang.

The Golden Range produced many strange characters, good, bad and indifferent, and I think of Curley of being a fair example of all these. Hailing from the ranks of the Texas Rangers he had some ten or twelve notches on his gun...'not countin' Indians and Negroes'. Hence, he always slept with one eye open, like all those of his kind.

Living in the country at that time was a rancher by the name of Spangler, John Spangler... a man badly crippled with rheumatism... who

Chapter 28: Curley

always carried a crutch about with him in his buggy when traveling.

Now it seemed that, somewhere in the list of Curley's enemies there was a man, in much the same condition as Spangler, who had sworn to kill him. None of us knew this until an odd circumstance brought it to light.

One autumn day on Pap's ranch there on the Walnut, Uncle Gil, Curley and myself were stacking feed in the yard back of the dugout barn in the creek bank when we saw a buggy approaching.

The ford was some three or four hundred yards to the north of the barn and feed lot where we were working.. After crossing the creek from the west, the road turned south and came up along the hillside directly in front of the barn. Therefore, Curley and I had a splendid view of anyone who crossed the ford and came up the road.

Curley took one look at the oncoming buggy, its-crippled driver and the Winchester beside the man, then quietly slid off the lead of feed. Drawing the ever ready six-shooter from his belt, he ran to the corner of the barn and waited for the buggy to round the wall.

Knowing the mistake in Curley's mind, Gil yelled, "Curley, you damn fool, that man's name is Spangler! I know him personally!"

Pale but calm, Curley put away his gun. A couple of minutes later, he shook hands with a somewhat mystified Spangler, who had seen Curley shove his gun back into his belt.

"Well, I just didn't aim to let that son-of-a-bitch get the drop on me," Curley explained. "He's plain poison with that Winchester of his. An' Spangler here looked just like him, riding in that damned buggy!"

The summer Uncle Gil worked for Curley on the ranch at Endee, Curley made his wife a present of a fine new six-shooter… one of those fancy pearl handle affairs Colt was making in those days. Being very

Chapter 28: Curley

proud of the gun, Mrs. Hatcher was standing in the back of the store, looking it over and admiring its shining metal and pearly handles.

It was summer and several, barefooted Mexican sheepherders, as well as others of the neighborhood, were lounging about in the cool of the 'dobe store. Seated on a keg of nails near the door was a big, swarthy Mexican named Pedro.

"Bet a dollar you can't hit my toe, Senora!" he called to the woman in the back of the store. Poking his foot out into the light from the oven door, he wiggled his toe tantalizingly.

The woman's reaction was instantaneous. The little gun flashed for an instant in the subdued light, cracked spitefully. The Mexican gave an astonished yell and then ran, howling, into the sunlit yard... minus a toe! Before he hobbled away to his shack to have his foot bandaged, his gleeful companions made him pay off his bet... a dollar to the lady of the gun!

A crack shot with either rifle, shotgun or six-shooter, Curley insisted his children and womenfolk learn the art as well. How well they learned the Mex was to remember the rest of his life.

One day in the wagon yard in front of the Endee store, Uncle Gil had a chance to witness Curley's splendid marksmanship. Mamie, Curley's little girl, had wandered off a way from the store's dooryard. Suddenly, a big longhorn steer spotted her. Lowering his head, he charged the child, head on! With a scream, Mamie dashed for the store. Inside, Curley heard her cry and rushed to the door. Already the terrible horns were sweeping toward Mamie's little body! Curley drew and fired, the bullet almost parting Mamie's golden curls. The longhorn dropped, the slug buried in its brain.

Curley had many guns, all of them of the finest makes. I still have his old double barrel Colt's shotgun... with which he claimed to have killed

Chapter 28: Curley

twelve men. Curley insisted it was the first shotgun the Colt's people ever made. Wishing a powerful gun for his work as a Ranger, he conceived the weapon and had it made to order.

More than half a century ago, my father bought the gun from Curley for forty dollars. With it came a reloading outfit and one hundred brass shells. A ten gauge, the thing was a powerful piece of ordinance. Loaded with #9 buckshot, it would kill a bear at a hundred yards... a feat Curley said he had accomplished several times in his life. Personally, I killed jackrabbits and prairie chicken with #4 shot at that distance on numerous occasions. When rightly loaded, the gun had a terrific recoil... enough to bruise a man's shoulder if not firmly held or knock a boy flat on his back.

Always a great story teller, Curley usually drew a crowd of listeners about him when he had time on his hands. His scouting days and his Texas Ranger background provided him with a never ending source of narrative. A collection of all the yarns he told us would make a big book in itself.

My Mother always said he was a big wind-bag, but, generally, he was very consistent in the telling of his stories. Repetition never led to any confusion. Several times I heard him tell the story of the white pacer that Frank Dobie recounts in his book, The Mustang. In both his accounts to me and to Dobie, the facts of the story are very much the same.

Being from the South, Curley was superstitious to the last degree. Hence, many of his stories were of ghosts and goblins and the many things pertaining to life and death for which he could not logically account.

One story centered around a haunted house where Curley or some of his companions had killed an outlaw whom they had surprised eating his lunch in an inner room. The killer, whichever one of them it was, had come up unexpectedly and seen the outlaw through the two doors of the

Chapter 28: Curley

house... and shot him.

After the killing, when the dead man had been removed, the inner door, for some unknown reason, refused to stay shut. No manner of latching or locking kept the door closed very long. After hearing of the incident, Curley made a special trip himself to the house. He tried everything... what others had tried before him, and things they hadn't tried. None of them worked. The door would not stay closed. Finally, angered and a little desperate, he secured it with heavy nails. The following morning, he returned, confident that the nails had solved the problem. In the doorway, he froze, suddenly chilled.

The door was standing wide open as usual; the big, hard-driven spikes protruding from the oak surface.

Another favorite story of Curley's centered around the splendid Winchester rifle which he had used in killing a horse thief. The shot had been fired at close range and blood from the falling man had spattered over the new rifle. Before Curley could wipe them off, those drops of blood ate right through the barrel of the gun, completely ruining it. Curley contended he kept this rifle for many years to show the potency of the blood of the men with whom he had to deal!

Not much given to religion as it was known and practiced then, he was yet zealous of other fellows ideas along those lines. He always insisted his victims be allowed to say their prayers before being hanged... all except a horse thief. Those characters, he felt, had no chance with God anyway... so why should a Ranger bother with them?

Sometimes, perhaps, he carried his zealous defense of others' religious beliefs almost too far. At an early age, his son, Henry, had learned to ask 'blessing' at the family table. Once a hungry plainsman barely escaped with his life at Curley's hands for beginning to eat before the boy had finished saying grace.

Chapter 28: Curley

Generally Pantheistic in his belief, Curley, nonetheless, contended that he had been a buffalo bull in some former state of existence and would probably, when he left this life again take on that form in his next reincarnation.

He could remember quite well, so he said, the glorious freedom he had enjoyed in his former life. He told of the great fight he had when the herds came together on the plains, of the many cows of his harem, of the lush grass of the prairies in the summer and of the blizzards weathered in the winters. His general appearance as a man certainly seemed to give credence to these ideas, for I never looked upon him without thinking of some old buffalo bull. Especially as he grew older and more taciturn in his nature.

Curley stayed among us for six or seven years, living on the ranch... either in Pap's house or along the creek in a camp of his own. He liked the wide open places and was never quite so happy as when sleeping under the stars with a string of good horses grazing about him.

Although his children, Mamie and Henry, visited him one summer, his wife apparently divorced him while he was still with us on the Golden Range. When he finally left our country, he took with him as wife the sister of an outlaw bunch who had terrorized the community for almost as long as he had been with us.

But, then, Curley always was different!

29. Tan, Lizzy and the Teater Kids

It had rained heavily the day before and now all the buffalo wallows and water holes in the draws were filled to overflowing. Late in the afternoon, Father and Mother loaded us kids in the back of the big wagon and started over the hill towards the north, heading for Bazine. At that time, Bazine was still up along what is now Highway 96; it was not until later that it was moved down along the railroad. Then roads didn't follow the section lines but, somewhat like the crow's flight, took the shortest route between places.

That old trail has long been obliterated in the furrows of Morey Brown's wheat field, and the huge buffalo wallow has long since been filled in and leveled down. But that day it was full. Full not only with water, but as we came over the hill onto the Dry Creek bottoms, it seemed with a laughing, shouting bunch of prairie children as well.

"Tan's kids," said my father, driving an down the hill and following the road into and across the big. lagoon.

There were eight or ten of the youngsters, both boys and girls, all dressed in makeshift bathing suits and having the time of their lives. Surrounding the wagon, they laughingly splashed the warm water of the lagoon all over us.

A little further on, we met a smiling prairie woman going, as she informed us, to "get them kids out of that water. They been in there the biggest part of the afternoon."

That was my introduction to the Teater kids and Lizzy, their mother. Later, I met 'old Tan', as everybody called him.

Big families were the order of the day on the Golden Range. And, I think, they were one of the prairie's greatest assets. If birth control had

Chapter 29: Tan, Lizzy and the Teater Kids

been practiced at that time, it would have taken a long while to settle up that vast country!

Four or five children was considered a small family, and eight or ten only an average. To do his duty, a man had to count twelve or fourteen at the least when roll call was made at meal time. Or at the going down of the sun. There were eight of us little Coles who lived to grow up. Two others died. Tan and Lizzy had twelve between them. Lizzy one, a boy by a former marriage, and Tan, six. Then there were five resulting from their own union.

"Yours and mine and ours," old Tan used to laughingly tell his wife.

At that time, the Teaters were living in a two room dugout in the bank of Dry Creek, a large branch of the Walnut that came down from the northwest out of the Chalk Hills and emptied its intermittent floods into the main creek just south of town. These prairie streams were much prettier then than at a later time. Their banks were covered with a fine growth of bushes and shrubbery... with many old trees scattered along their winding ways. Great quantities of wild plum and chokeberry grew there, as well as wild fox grape and currant and hackberry. It was a wilderness of beauty where the old dugout had its place. An ideal locality for such a boisterous bunch of healthy, happy savages such as Tan and Lizzy tried to keep in line.

Like all the rest of that first generation of Golden Range children, the Teater kids were dependent upon their own ingenuity for their amusement. And with nothing in the world to hinder them, they went about it with such a right good will that it was accomplished almost before they began.

That summer of 1886 was a wet one on the prairies. It was a common sight to see Tan's bunch in the big lagoon almost any time of the

Chapter 29: Tan, Lizzy and the Teater Kids

day. Later that fall, a big flood came rolling down the Dry Creek and the Teaters had to find other lodgings.

One often wonders why those early day men had to always learn the hard way, where to build their homes. That old dugout, when I first became acquainted with the Teater family, had its threshold flush with the bottom of the creek. One had only to note the drift wood high up in the forks of the trees to realize the consequences of a wet season. But with the wet seasons rare... and the making of a dugout no small chore... the few months security beneath its dirt roof compensated for the risks.

At any rate, the Teaters moved out that fall with barely time enough between the rain and the flood to salvage their household stuff. However, with the prairie level being only a few feet back of the dugout, they pulled back there with no real loss. Afterward, Tan and Lizzy began looking for another nest for the brood.

My next memory of the family was when I started to school at the age of six. My father had moved north of town that winter, close to some wheat fields that promised good winter pasture. He had contracted with a rancher out on the Forrester to feed a bunch of horses for him that winter. And since Rube Reynolds and his father had departed for Colorado, Father rented their place, along with the wheat, and we moved in.

It was my first term of school. My older sister and I walked a mile and a half to the stone school house in the north part of town. There, we again encountered the Teater tribe who were to play such an important part in our 'growing up years. Tan had moved them from the dugout in the bank of the creek to a house in old Bazine. Most of the older ones attended school that first winter, I know... for it was at this time that memory began to record them in my mind.

Very distinctly, I recall my first attack of puppy love which overwhelmed me the following spring. The object of my so soon aroused

Chapter 29: Tan, Lizzy and the Teater Kids

passion? Effie, the then youngest of the Teater girls. However, since there were some forty or fifty other prairie flowers attending the school, my great love quickly waned... only to flare up in another direction. For no sooner had I enticed Effie and her girl friend into a corner of the school playground than I forgot Effie and fell in love with her girl friend! How inconsistent we mortals be! Afterward, Effie was always the boon companion and much respected compatriot in many a childhood escapade... but never again an amoretto!

Shortly after this, the Teater family moved again; this time back to another dugout in the bank of the main creek. This was the dugout old Eli Wolf had excavated just a mile downstream from the Cole layout. Here the Teaters lived for some time.

Old Tan went to work as section foreman on the new railroad running through Bazine. The section of the road for which he was responsible extended four miles each way from the section house in Bazine. Six days a week he worked, ten hours a day, for a dollar and a quarter a day. And the job a coveted one in the business! The men under him... those who drove the spikes and hauled the dirt... received a dollar a day and a very generous portion of old Tan's Scotch-Irish vocabulary. Being an ex-soldier from the Union side, he hired only Union men to begin with. But as we got farther and farther away from Appomattox, he became more mellow. Almost any man with a reasonable amount of energy could call him 'boss'. Even a Mexican, a class not much tolerated on the plains.

Probably it was because Pap Cole had served in the Mexican War that he and Tan got along so well together. Tan received all of twelve dollars a month from the government for whipping Pap and his companions into line; Pap got eight dollars a month for whipping the Mexicans and almost doubling Uncle Sam's domain. So it more or less evened out. They never had any trouble between them, and many a

Chapter 29: Tan, Lizzy and the Teater Kids

Christmas dinner Tan and Lizzy ate at Pap's table.

The spring following the horse feeding venture, my father moved the family south of town onto the Ross Lawrence or Herrington places. Herrington was, I believe, a brother-in law to Ross Lawrence. He and Lawrence had gained title to a considerable body of land lying up and down the creek in that locality. It was good creek bottom land and Father immediately purchased what we always called the 'home quarter', and began the accumulation of the thousand or more acres that were to become the body of his ranch. Two miles up the creek, Pap and the other boys were similarly occupied gaining title to the land that made up the old Cole ranch.

In those days, the Coles had control of several thousand acres lying along the creek and south almost to the divide between the Pawnee and the Walnut. Pap also had access to and ran his cattle over a considerable strip of country north and west of the old ranch house in the bank of the creek.

My father could not go very far north with his cattle because of the little town of Bazine which had sprung up on the southwest quarter of the old Farnsworth place. A few years later, Farnsworth and his outfit moved into Arizona. For years after, we had access to his holdings and quite frequently ranged our stock east and north along the creek. The Golden Range was a big country and since the land had little value, save for the grass, we were somewhat careless as to who held title to the land. The 'Boom' had burst and the thousands who had formed the bubble had evaporated into other parts... leaving the mortgage companies of the east with the paper.

Across the creek, about half a mile north and west of our new home, lived a family by the name of Miller. Dave Miller and his wife, Lucy. The Millers had four or five children about the same age as the Cole

Chapter 29: Tan, Lizzy and the Teater Kids

and Teater broods. But like many other Golden Range people, the Millers were drifters. They didn't tarry long in the new frame house Dave had moved from town onto his land. Just long enough to leave a void in the neighborhood when they moved away.

True to my earlier inclinations, I developed a great crush for Dottie, the youngest of the Miller girls, at ten years of age. Strong emotion always leaves a deep impression, and at that time, I was at a very impressionable age. The night before the Millers moved away from the Golden Range, Dottie and I spent an hour or more in the back of their covered wagon, consoling one another and swearing eternal fidelity to the love that was consuming our young natures. Beautiful puppy love! How divine are its pangs... and how eternal. I cannot speak for Dot, but I do know that I have remained faithful to the vows of that evening. I have never forgotten.

Shortly after the Millers vacated the new house on the bank of the creek, old Tan moved his bunch down there, ushering in a new beginning of a long and happy era for all of us.

There never lived, in any land, a better or more neighborly couple than Tan and Lizzy Teater!

30. Along the Creek

The years since 1876 had gone by in a great hurrah and now, ten years later, Pap Cole and his wife, Susan although still active members of prairie society... were beginning to show the halting hand of time.

Despite this gradual slowing down, Grandmother continued to keep house for 'Mr. Cole', as she always insisted on calling him. Jake, Gil and Jim were still at home, as was Effie Lee, but all the other children had scattered out over the Golden Range, making homes for themselves.

Pap had changed, the fires of ambition small, cool flames now. In the summer, he sat, his chair tilted back against the east wall of the house, and looked off over the eastern hills... dreaming of Virginia and Shenandoah and the days of his youth. In the winter, he spent a great deal of the day in an easy chair near the huge, wood-burning stove in the living room. The boys managed to keep him well supplied with wood from the creek and the visiting countryside made his days pass pleasantly enough. By this time, his prophecy of the golden wheat fields had, in a measure, been fulfilled. Although the Coles were all stockmen and, hence, most of the creek bottoms were still held as grazing land, wheat fields had begun to spot the prairies... and Pap insisted the days of the big herds were numbered.

With the coming of Tan and Lizzy and their boisterous, happy bunch to the house across the creek, a new day was ushered in for us on the old Herrington place. The Cole girls had companions now, and we boys teamed up in a fine way with the Teater boys.

From the first day of their coming, until the day almost twenty years later when they moved away, a day never passed that did not find, somewhere in its golden hours, the Cole and Teater kids associated in some youth adventure. Mother used to often declare that she scarcely

Chapter 30: Along the Creek

knew which were 'hers' and which were 'Lizzie's'. And Old Tan, when in need of help, would issue orders to a Cole as quickly as to a Teater.

The older Teater girls early became school teachers, all five of them, but when school was over or a holiday came around, we were continually together. There were three of the younger boys in old Tan's bunch, just as there were three in Father's corral, and there was never a day passed that we were not together. Riding, hunting, fishing, swimming, skating on the creeks in the winter time... or herding the cattle and horses out on the miles of free range that surrounded the old ranch house.

This feeling of close kinship, to a lesser degree, extended to the grown-ups. For instance, Father bargained for the old Miller homestead, intending to add this very desirable quarter section to his already growing range. But when Tan expressed a wish to purchase it for a home, Father turned it over to his much desired neighbor.

Thus it was with the Coles and the Teaters on the Golden Range. There we grew up, and there memory most often returns.

Then, as now, the creek was a fairy land of beauty and romance in a somewhat prosaic country side. Not that the prairies weren't beautiful; they were... even when the summer's sun and the hot dry winds had drawn away most of their green. But the creek was always green in season, and, in the winter time, a wilderness of trees and brush that offered escape from the biting, bone-chilling winds. Like a gigantic serpent, it wound its sensuous way, for a hundred miles or more across the greater part of the Golden Range. A cool, delightful retreat in summer, a warm, sheltered place in winter.

The Cole and Teater kids knew every swimming hole within a fifty mile radius. Other things we knew, too. Where the best plums and chokeberries, the choicest fox grapes and black currants could be found. Hackberries one need not hunt for; they grew everywhere. Fishing was

Chapter 30: Along the Creek

great; one had only to cast a baited hook into the water almost anywhere to get a strike.

In the winter, when the miles and miles of water were frozen over, great skating parties were organized. Young people from miles around gathered either at the Cole ranch or over at the Teater place. From there they hurried to the creek where, lost in its sheltered depths, they skated away the long hours of a winter's night. At every bend along its length, we built huge bonfires (dry wood was plentiful) and, every so often, we had a chicken roasting or a pot of beans simmering... along with plenty of hot coffee.

In the fall, hog killing time was always a neighborhood affair. My father owned a great steel vat, one which he had secured when the old sugar mill at Ness City burned. In this we heated water for scalding the hogs. Sometimes, these hog killings would last for two or three days, many neighbors bringing their hogs to our place for the killing and cleaning. On the nights following such butchering, we young people would slip off across the creek with a great quantity of tenderloin and other choice portions of pork. These barbecues often lasted half the night.

Like Uncle Jim before us, we Cole boys... and the Teater boys as well...knew where most of the melon patches of the countryside were, as well as the time of their ripening.

Old Tan was a great story teller, and the oft repeated tales of his own boyhood escapades seemed to lend a certain license for his boys to do likewise. Consequently, most of our forays were less amateurish than might have been expected.

As a general rule, a melon patch was considered common property. Therefore, with reasonable care as to the vines and fences, most of the settlers paid little attention to our forays. Quite frequently the girls would accompany us on the less complicated raids. But those requiring ingenuity

Chapter 30: Along the Creek

and a certain amount of skill were generally engineered by the older boys. Afterward, we rendezvoused down along the creek bank, where the girls shared our booty.

Certain settlers, however, put up at least a token resistance against these raids. One such character, Hilgar Shaben, lived over on the divide some five or six miles south of the creek. Now Mr. Shaben was a very frugal soul, although by no means stingy, and he always had a big melon patch in season. No doubt had we asked for melons, he would have given them to us. But it seemed like Hilgar's melons always tasted better when we stole them out of the patch.

Quite frequently, our parents sent us to purchase melons from Hilgar and, in so doing, we had ample opportunity to spy out the land. A big draw came up alongside the patch, which was almost a quarter of a mile from Hilgar's dugout. This afforded excellent protection, and tended to make us more daring than usual.

In the course of the summer, we made several very successful raids on the patch... until Hilgar, becoming wise to our methods, virtually put an end to things. Whenever one of us rode into the neighborhood of the melon patch, Hilgar usually appeared with an old musket cradled in the crook of his arm. Even an idiot would have taken the hint; we were not idiots.

One Sunday morning, after bringing our cattle onto the range about a mile west of the patch, we tied our horses to some scrubby trees in plain sight of the dugout. Our plan was simple. While Hilgar thought we were resting in the shade of the trees along with the horses, we would raid the melon patch from the shelter of the draw.

It seemed fortune favored this scheme. For after crawling almost half a mile on our hands and knees along the bottom of the draw, we emerged undetected, alongside the melon patch. Hilgar was nowhere in

Chapter 30: Along the Creek

sight. With near professional efficiency, we rolled several of the larger melons over the bank and out of sight of the dugout. Once safely away from the place, we ate our ill-gotten loot... congratulating ourselves on how we had so cleverly outwitted old Hilgar Shaben.

The gay, overconfidence of youth!

Returning to the trees an hour later, our laughter stilled in our throats. One of the Teater horses was missing. The saddle and bridle were neatly piled together near the other animals; only the saddle rope was gone. A single glance toward the Shaben ranch told us the story. The missing horse was nibbling hay in an outdoor manger in the corral back of the barn.

While we had, in truth, been stealing Hilgar's melons the old man had, symbolically, 'stolen' one of our horses!

There wasn't a thing we could do about it. Not one of us had the courage to go and claim the horse. For Hilgar knew we had not been innocently resting in the shade of the trees... and none of us cared to find out just what he would do about those missing melons. So, doubling up on one of the other horses, we finished the day and drove the herds back to the ranch.

Naturally, we had no intention of telling the folks about our ill-fated raid. But just how to account for the missing horse posed a tricky problem. Belatedly, Fortune smiled upon us. For arriving at the creek, we found it bank full from a roaring flood. Somewhere up stream there had been a big rain and the flood waters were just now getting down our way.

Now the Teater cattle had to cross the creek to reach their home corral. It was a tricky job, but the Teater boys did it well. Fording the reluctant cattle into the water with whistling ropes, the boys drove them across the creek... swimming behind them to keep them going. In this

Chapter 30: Along the Creek

matter of swimming, they had no choice, their one remaining horse refusing to take the water. Turned loose on our side of the creek, this ornery critter gave the Teater boys the alibi they so desperately needed. For when old Tan inquired about the horses they had a very plausible story an the tips of their tongues.

The blamed horses had refused to cross the creek at flood stage!

Some two weeks later, we found the horse, Bob, running loose on the prairie. Old man Shaben, despairing of our claiming him and no doubt becoming weary of feeding and watering him, had turned him loose.

The incident was one more lesson in the process of growing up.

You are never quite as smart as you think you are!

31. A Day's Work

For three days, without interruption, the great herd rumbled past the ranch house in that spring of '91... snorting, bellowing, clicking their incredible spread of horns. Mile after mile of longhorns moving on over the divide toward the north... while local cattlemen fought to keep their own cattle pulled back from the line of march, and the trail drive cowboys did everything they could to keep the settler's cattle from mixing with the big herd.

Three full days, and then the last of them were gone forever, leaving behind only the hoove rutted land and slow settling dust to mark their passage.

Although only a little fellow at the time, I remember with what fascination I watched the seemingly endless string of longhorns moving over the prairies. History has recorded this drive, and my father knew the man who made it. But I have long since forgotten their names. My memory embraces, however, the cattle... thousands upon thousands of them... stretching south toward the Pawnee and north toward the divide that dips down to the Bigtimber and the Dry Creek.

The records will tell the story of the herd boss who started north with three thousand longhorn cattle, his destination the Black Hills. They will also reveal how he bought two more herds of three thousand head each and hired the men of each outfit to help him on through. That was the largest single herd of cattle ever to cross the Golden Range country under one management. Each herd had its own outfit and herd boss, but one man owned the entire lot of almost ten thousand head. And one man carried the roll back with him when they were finally sold in the Black Hills country of the Dakotas! They did things in a big way on the Golden Range!

They are still doing things in a big way, but it is no longer cattle that move over the prairies. Combines and wheat trucks and transcontinental coaches and little men under big management and the world moves on! The cattle go to market on wheels and in a different direction, and the Indian gets his meat in a tin instead of on foot as in the days of his greatness. Yet it is still difficult for me to forget the old ways.

We had several longhorn cattle in our herds when I first began to lead them out to graze on the prairies... calves that were left behind by the trail herds moving north.

"Take this one along, sonny," the wrangler used to tell me. "Feed him an old Bossy's milk an' he'll make a good cow some day." 'He' or 'she' was always 'he' with the old-time cowboy when speaking of a calf, but that made no difference with the rancher if old Bossy was agreeable.

Sheep were not tolerated on our part of the Golden Range. Only once was a considerable number ever seen in those parts and they were rushed past as fast as their short legs could carry them. To make certain of this, a number of ranchers rode along, determined to get rid of the 'outrage' as quickly as possible. For several months afterward, our cattle refused to eat the grass in that part of the country. And for almost two years we could tell the trail of the sheep by the length of the grass. For almost as many years, we boys used the dried pellets of sheep manure for sling shot ammunition.

As the days of the great herds slowly drew to a close, the problems of the cattleman became more and more complicated. When the Coles first founded their ranches along the Walnut the range was almost unlimited, and they rounded up their cattle only to brand, and get a count of the herds when they were ready to market.

The 'Boom' broke in upon these halcyon days for a short period, but its hours were soon spent. Once more the prairies returned to their quiet glory. There were those who felt that the situation would remain thus

Chapter 31: A Day's Work

forever. But Pap Cole insisted that nothing remained unchanged, and that this period of tranquility was only, a breathing spell. He, therefore, cautioned his boys to make friends with the settlers and farmers who stayed over from that hectic period marking the 'Boom'... as well as those who began to slowly fill up the ranks of the departed.

"There are just too many people needing bread in the east," he said. "And too many good farmers in those parts without land to think that rich country like this will be allowed to grow only buffalo grass very long."

In this Pap was right for the range began to slowly spot itself with the homes of new settlers. Not as in the boom days, one on every quarter section, but slowly, here and there... sometimes many miles apart.

There was one marked difference between these later settlers and the original 'Boomers'! The manner of their coming, the nature of their belongings and the homes which they built. The 'Boomer' made himself a soddy or a dugout and secured his patent from the U.S. Land Office. The newcomer went to the county seat and came away with a deed to the land, signed by an eastern mortgage company who had acquired it from the original homesteader. Also, he brought back to his place a big load of lumber for the new farm house that would soon dot the prairie.

The free grass was the same, but the effort to get to it and to protect the newcomer added greatly to the cattleman's worries. Horseflesh became more valuable, especially saddle stock, for the herds must be followed and the fields protected... even though they were widely scattered. The cattlemen went into Texas and brought up X.I.T. horses, or into Idaho for bunchgrass stock, and trained their young men to handle the restless cattle... for herdsmen were scarce.

When I was fourteen, I got my first job as a 'professional' cowboy. My employer, Uncle Jim.

Chapter 31: A Day's Work

"Gavit has offered me six hundred head of cattle to pasture this summer at twenty cents per head per month," he told me. "Now I won't be home very much. But if you want a job, I'll give you fifteen dollars a month to handle 'em for me...an' you can stay here with Pap and ma. What do you say?"

"You got yourself a man," I replied promptly. Almost too promptly; for fifteen dollars was a princely sum to a boy only fourteen years old. Besides I would not be needed at home until corn cutting time in the fall.

Shortly afterward, the cattle were driven onto the range by Gavit riders, my uncle turned over four good horses to me, my bed roll was brought to the ranch... and I was on my own.

"You can water them in the Pawnee or here in the Walnut," Uncle Jim said. "An' then there is the well on the divide. Keep the well going, with plenty of water in the tank, an' they won't be too restless. They're a bunch of outlaws, them longhorns! Used to runnin' all over west Texas. An' don't kid yourself; they'll be tryin' to get back there before the summer's over! Just remember one thing... we'll have to give old Gavit a proper head count this fall or dig in our pockets an' pay for the shortage. If one dies cut out the brand and save it. It'll count same as a live steer."

Riding out on the range that first day with that bunch of Texas cattle, I really felt tall in the saddle. For these were longhorns of the old stock, wild as antelope and as dangerous as a rattlesnake. Since I had complete say about them, the responsibility weighed heavily upon me. I was grimly determined that nothing should happen to them.

With the matter satisfactorily settled, Uncle Jim went away to some other work, leaving me with my needle-horned companions. There was no need for worry. The grass was there, and the water... if it lasted, and the horseflesh. All I had to do was ride; and ride I did... sometimes

Chapter 31: A Day's Work

eighteen and twenty hours a day. A fresh horse every morning for four days, and then back to the first one. Sometimes, I felt as though another boy, as well, would have been welcome. But none came, and I rode the summer away with no help from anyone.

Learning the habits of my cattle helped ease the burden of my work. When I bedded them down at night I always knew when and where I would find them in the morning. If the weather was fair, they generally remained where I left them. But if a storm came up in the night, I had to stay with them or they would have been scattered to the four winds by morning. One night during a storm I lost forty head and did not find them for almost a week. That was a very busy time for both me and the horses! Not only did I have to ride over a hundred square mile area searching for the lost cattle, but I also had to keep track of where the main herd was grazing.

On the fifth day, I rode upon the strays, grazing in a wild hay meadow beside a prairie stream, many miles south of the home range. Had I been a man, I would have cursed them soundly; being a boy, I was simply happy to find them safe. After returning them to the main herd, it took two or three days to get them reinstated into the group. To accomplish this, I had to be up early and late. Before it was over, I was worn to a frazzle.

The following morning, I rode to the top of a slight rise about half a mile from the main herd and stretching out in the shadow of my horse, with my jacket for a pillow, I fell asleep from sheer exhaustion. How long I slept, I don't know; it didn't seem very long. Suddenly, I snapped awake, the snorting and bellowing of the herd loud in my ears.

Even before I opened my eyes, I sensed my danger. One quick look confirmed my fears. Completely surrounding me as I lay stretched out there on the grass was a shoving, snorting herd of longhorns! The nearest of the vicious animals was almost within goring distance! Luckily,

Chapter 31: A Day's Work

however, curiosity seemed to dominate them for the moment. Those closest to me kept sniffing and crowding around, trying to figure out what I was and just what to do about it.

For a moment, I lay there, my heart pounding, trying to figure out an escape. Only too well I knew the temperament of these longhorns. Many a cowboy, caught in just such a predicament, had died under their pounding hoofs and needle-tipped horns. My only hope was my horse... and my horse was nowhere in sight. Still, I knew that he was somewhere there beyond the shifting, grunting cattle. Somehow, I had to get to him.

Cautiously, I slipped my hands up alongside my head and grasped the jacket I had been using as a pillow. Then, taking a deep breath, I jack-knifed to my feet, waving the jacket wildly about me and shouting at the top of my voice! For just an instant, the cattle scattered in fright giving me a glimpse of my horse grazing quietly a few hundred yards in front of me. I ran toward him like a scared deer. Luck was with me. Swinging into the saddle, I raced away... bare yards ahead of the nearest steer snorting at my heels! That was probably the closest brush with death I've ever had.

As I've said, the responsibility for the herd weighed somewhat heavily upon me. To say the least, I took my job seriously… as a certain cattleman soon found out.

Bert Ellis, a rancher living several miles up the creek, had also contracted to graze a like number of cattle under the same conditions as Uncle Jim. One day, while riding around my herd I saw a rider working in and out among them, giving them a careful once over. A few days before, a couple of longhorns had come into my herd which I suspected of being Ellis' strays. I had marked them well in my mind, expecting them to be claimed sooner or later. So I had a pretty good idea what the fellow was looking for.

Riding over, I asked him who he was and what he wanted. He said

Chapter 31: A Day's Work

he was from the Ellis ranch and was looking for strays.

"Got any in your herd?" he asked.

"Yelp," I said, boy-like and not thinking. "Got a couple."

"Well, I'm short two," he replied. "So I'll just take two out of your bunch and get goin."

"No," I said. "You'll take your two an' no other."

"What's the difference which ones I take," he exclaimed.

"They are all Gavit cattle. Just so you have your right amount an' I have mine this fall is all old Gavit cares about. Same as me, he won't know one from another."

"Well, I know the difference," I informed him firmly. "An' you will have to know before you take any cattle out of my herd."

"Ah, come on, kid," he said. "You pick 'em... any ones you want to... an' I'll take 'em along."

"I ain't pickin' nothin' out. If you don't know your own cattle, that's your hard luck. I know mine, an' I intend to keep 'em. Besides, I just might lose some between now an' fall. Them two of yours might come in handy to make up my loss."

By now, the rider's patience had begun to wear thin. He insisted he was going to take two head out of my herd no matter what. He probably would have, too, if I hadn't started to the ranch after Uncle Jim. Evidently not wanting to tangle with my uncle, he rode away... cursing softly about a stubborn kid who knew more than his elders.

I was two steers long that fall when we counted back to Gavit. Ellis was two short.

That entire summer, the well on the divide was my chief worry.

Chapter 31: A Day's Work

My struggles with it were almost continuous. It was forty feet deep with a twenty foot windmill tower over it. The pipe through which the water was lifted to the surface was a one and a quarter inch galvanized affair in three foot sections. At the bottom was a brass cylinder with leather valves. Sand in the well cut out these valves about every three weeks. Then it became necessary to pull the pipes and replace the valves. This job I had to do with no help save my saddle horse and two or three lengths of saddle rope.

A pulley in the tower above the well and a rope through this, half hitched around the pipe and the saddle horn at the far end of the rope, was my working equipment. I had one horse that was a good puller from the saddle horn. Fastening him to the running end of the rope, all I had to do was tell him to go and the pipe came up until I called 'Stop'. Securing the pipe with another piece of rope, I uncoupled it with two more short pieces of rope and two sticks. The inner or sucker rod was uncoupled with a monkey wrench and a pair of pliers.

Late in the summer, the creek went dry and I was hard put to find water for the thirsty herd. Pap insisted I look along the banks of the now dry creek and if I found a place where there was a growth of bull-rushes to dig there. This I did. To my amazement, a huge stream of water gushed out and filled all the low places in the channel for nearly a mile downstream!

It was a busy summer, and I was glad when the Gavit men came in the fall and took the longhorns away. I looked forward to the corn-cutting at home as a vacation!

Epilogue

The mill of the gods grinds slowly, but only they who dare bring their grist to the mill may know the texture of the grinding.

Pap Cole had dared to look down the years, and prophetic eyes had granted him a satisfying vision. He passed over the disagreeable, the discouraging... if there was such for him... and saw only the fulness of his dreams. The Golden Range and its peoples, a completed day... a finished entente.

The Mason-Dixon line of his youth had forever passed away. 'Reb' and 'Yankee' were obsolete terms, used only to recall the past, and, then, with no rancor of memory. The Mississippi and the Congo were rapidly mingling their waters... if not physically, certainly intellectually. The word 'slave' had disappeared forever from the vocabulary of the Golden Range... regardless of how Effie Lee had tried to retain it. 'Ni***r', too, was gone; the black men had become 'colored'. Cheyenne, Comanche, Sioux had merged into American. 'South Ireland' had long ago become High Point Township, and 'North Ireland', the McCraken neighborhood.

A vast era was rapidly drawing to a close.

Contentment is the end of human endeavor. Pap knew that... and was a trail blazer. Cane in hand, like Oll and Knappy and their wagons, he went on over the divide, following a new trail into a new land.

"I am not afraid of this," he told his son, John, as he lay dying. "One morning, long ago, we shot Billy Mitchell for desertion... down in the Gila Bend country. But I ain't no deserter, even though I'll be goin' on pretty soon now.

"Clear my mouth out, will you, John. Always knew I'd die rich. Now, see? Can't even spit off my own property!

Epilogue

"Susan, give Ira my old hat. He won it a long time ago in a foot race. I won't be needin' it anymore."

And then he was gone, and a way of life with him. Yet a part of him lived on in the land which he had helped to pioneer... and which he had loved so deeply.

My father died a few years later, trading horses to the very end. The Golden Range lost a great plainsman with his passing. One of the greatest, in my opinion.

Cass, Gil, Jim, Jake... all went the same year, following one another in rapid succession. And the last of that generation of Cole men were gone forever. The old neighbors, most of them, who endured pain and hardships and loneliness that coming generations might live in a land of peace and plenty... they, too, have gone. Never will the world know a sturdier breed of men, nor suffer a greater love!

My mother, at one hundred and two, and Aunt Nancy, Gil's wife, at eighty-five, still carry on... the last of the Cole women. The story rapidly draws to a close, but memory and tradition in the second and third generations still bring to life the old days... especially at Christmas time.

A great many of us Coles are glad today that Pap ever followed Kearney into the southwest!

With the passing of the men of that day, a mighty era in American history was brought to a close. A whole day, I like to think. Both the evening and the morning and the day was complete... with never another day like it in all time.

A scripture in Genesis sums it up magnificently:

"There were giants in the earth in those days!"

The prophet might well have been looking down to this day when

Epilogue

he wrote those words. And, to finish the quotation:

"And also after that, when the sons of God came in unto the daughters of men, the same became mighty men which were of old, men of renown."

Yes, they were giants, those men who claimed and conquered the Golden Range. Spiritually, I like to think that their women Mary-like, conceived from divine intercourse. Surely the travail of their souls were required of them when they brought forth a breed of beings hardy enough to tame the wilderness of that new world in which they found themselves.

The Golden Range country has changed. Old landmarks have passed away. When I would recall 'Yesterday', I must close my eyes and rely on memory to bring back the vision. For ten thousand grain elevators, dotting the countryside, tell today where the freight wagons went. In an hours time one crossed the miles from Dodge to Hays; a distance it took the freight wagons three days to travel in Pap's time. The trails, unlike then, run along the section lines... straight, well graded, surveyed. 'Yesterday', we followed the lines of least resistance, traveling two or three together in order to double up on the rough places. Our guide posts? A lone tree on the divide. A pile of rock, like John's Folly. Little things, but so vitally important. A thousand trees today for every one then, and the stones have been moved to make way for the plow and the tractor. Still--

Because of memory we are men. I am glad I am a man!

****

Boulder, Colorado

September 5, 1961

By - Ira Cole

www.ingramcontent.com/pod-product-compliance
Lightning Source LLC
Chambersburg PA
CBHW031441040426
42444CB00007B/922